I'm Judging You

I'm Judging You

You

The Do-Better Manual

Luvvie Ajayi

A HOLT PAPERBACK   HENRY HOLT AND COMPANY   NEW YORK

Holt Paperbacks
Henry Holt and Company, LLC
Publishers since 1866
175 Fifth Avenue
New York, New York 10010
www.henryholt.com

Library of Congress Cataloging-in-Publication Data

Names: Ajayi, Luvvie.
Title: I'm judging you : the do-better manual / Luvvie Ajayi.
Description: First edition | New York : Henry Holt and Company, [2016] |
   "A Holt paperback."
Identifiers: LCCN 2016009018 | ISBN 9781627796064 (paperback) |
   ISBN 9781627796071 (ebook)
Subjects: LCSH: Conduct of life—Humor. | BISAC: HUMOR / Form / Essays.
Classification: LCC PN6231.C142 A43 2016 | DDC 818.602—dc23
LC record available at https://lccn.loc.gov/2016009018

Our books may be purchased in bulk for promotional, educational, or business use. Please contact your local bookseller or the Macmillan Corporate and Premium Sales Department at (800) 221-7945, extension 5442, or by e-mail at MacmillanSpecialMarkets@macmillan .com.

First Edition 2016

Designed by Meryl Sussman Levavi

Printed in the United States of America

10   9

Contents

I'm Judging You

Introduction:
New Rules for a New World

 One day, I was minding everyone's business, scrolling through my Facebook news feed when I saw a picture of someone's dead grandma being prepared for burial. I gasped and then immediately got mad. *Who does that?* Why would you upload a snapshot of your deceased relative? What are you trying to prove? Because I'm pretty sure we didn't need to see receipts showing that she really died. We believe you. You didn't need any more people. Furthermore, why would you post a picture of her body before it's casket-sharp? Her wig wasn't even on yet. People are so disrespectful. I promise you this: if I die and someone posts a picture of my body before my lipstick is on and I'm looking amazing (for the state I'm in), I will haunt them for the rest of their lives. Ghost Luvvie would be turning on random faucets in their houses in the middle of the night. Anytime they ate popcorn, I'd hide all the floss so they'd have to live with that stuff stuck between their teeth. I am super petty.

Anyway, at times like this, when someone obviously lacks sense, you ask yourself, "Did some of us not get a limited-edition handbook with instructions on how not to suck? Was there a boot camp on decency that some people simply missed the sign-up for?" Why are people terrible? In a world where we are more connected to each other than ever, with endless access to information at our fingertips, too many of us seem to have missed the message on how to behave. Babies and grandmothers alike have Instagram pages—I've seen a five-year-old's Instagram, where he posted about naptime and coloring inside the lines. The Dalai Lama, the pope, and the president of the United States use Twitter to pass on messages to the masses. We are living in a new world, and there are now new rules. Information travels faster than ever, instantly exposing who is the emperor without clothes.

Clearly, we need a playbook, a guide to help people get a bit of common sense and some behavior as they navigate today's hyper-obsessions with pop culture, social-media sharing, and outright navel-gazing.

If Oprah and Deepak came up today, in a world where more people die in botched selfie attempts than in shark attacks, this might be the book they'd recommend. This book is what Millennial Iyanla Vanzant would give you before you get to the point where you have to go sit on her couch for fixing.

"If there's a book that you want to read, but it hasn't been written yet, then you must write it." Prolific writer Toni Morrison once said that. And so I have.

Here is where I dole out shade, side-eye, and basic-but-necessary advice for the needy—the logic-deficient who consistently come up short in this new world order of 140-character opinions, Facebook beefs, Instagram groupies, and pop-cultural idolization, i.e., the wasteland, where common sense has tragically become the rarest flower in the thought garden. *I'm Judging You* changes the game and snatches wigs one page at a time. It is a guide to getting some act-right online and in real life. All the shade that resides in my spirit, all the side-eye I've dispensed across my vast network, has led me here.

Life doesn't usually come with a manual, and we're all just going through it as best as we know how. We're hoping that when we follow the drinking gourd to our Lord and show up at Saint Peter's gate he doesn't turn us away for being terrible people who don't deserve nice things, like heaven's promises. I imagine heaven to be a place where I can afford any shoes I want, I can drink all the pink lemonade I can stand, and the pasta and shrimp are eternally endless. Also, roaches and rodents do not exist there because they are clearly Satan's minions and they belong in the burning basement of hell forever and ever. Amen.

But I digress.

Humans are flawed beings. Some flaws are mere wrinkles, some are cracks, and some are the Grand Canyon. This book will address everything from the quirks that earn my shallower-than-a-Snapple-cap gripes to the really problematic things people do that leave the world worse than we found it and inspire my wrath—from side-eyeing our beauty, hygiene, relationship, friendship, and everyday decisions to calling out oppression and inequality, phobia-driven social systems, and people's views on race, religion, and being different; to frowning at the endlessly wrong ways we're using digital platforms in our business and personal relationships; and finally, to wig-snatching the glorification of megalomania and the lowest-common-denominator pandering of social media and reality TV.

But who am I kidding? The truth is this book is an amazing excuse for me to judge folks. It's a permanent scowl in book form—a gift that'll sizzle on the shelves of the Library of Congress for generations to come.

I would like to take this time to acknowledge, praise, and lift up those judges who've come before me. The ones whose side-eye could break your spirit and whose words could cut you down to your socks. Shout-out to professional judges (Judy and Mathis) and to unofficial ones—like shady babies everywhere who give no dambs[1] about your feelings—and to Sophia Petrillo (my favorite Golden Girl). Also, shout-out to your grandmother and other old people in your life who say what they feel and dare you to check them. They all exist to ensure that we behave better, and for them I give thanks. Finally, a shout-out to my Nigerian mom, who taught me such insults as "classless wonder" and "useless nonentity." I am (shady) because they are.

I like to think of myself as ahead of my time because I'm already cranky and ornery, and I'm working toward getting a lawn just so I can chase people off it. I'm futuristic that way. Some people will say, "Only God can judge me." I'm here to say, "Well, until He gives His final judgment, here's some of mine."

You're welcome!

---

[1] *damb*: Because it's more fun than "damn." Get used to this.

PART

1

Life

We are all annoying and do assholish things every single day. Just think of the people who are sitting at the back of the plane, and the moment the flight lands they jump up. Ma'am, you are in seat 35G. WHERE ARE YOU GOING? There are 173 people in front of you, and they also cannot wait to get off. What are you about to do from your window seat in the back row? Will you magically appear in the front of the plane? No. Please have a seat, because your turn to deplane ain't coming for like ten good minutes.

Oh, people. We're the worst.

Gosh, You're the Worst

 There are some people who fall short in the "being thoughtful" department. They aren't being malicious, but they certainly tap-dance on people's last nerves with their shenanigans. These are the people who are perpetually late, take advantage of their friends in various ways, and children. We know them and love them and we keep them in our lives, but we sometimes wish that they would get their shit together.

There are two types of people in this world: people who can be on time and Nigerians. I am in the latter group, and I confess to my inability to arrive anywhere punctually. I am pretty sure I'll be late to my own funeral, doing a running jump into my casket like the inconsiderate jerk I am, right before the pastor tells everyone how awesome I was and the choir sings a rousing rendition of "I Luh God." Please tell everyone that the dress code is all red everything, and check with my best friend to see if you're on the list of people who aren't invited, because leave it up to me to be petty from the Great Beyond. If I didn't mess with you while I was here, I surely don't need to see your feet at my highly exclusive homegoing.

It really is terrible to be perpetually tardy for the party, and I am judging everyone who is, especially myself. I am the worst, like a stale Twizzler you find at the bottom of that purse you haven't carried in six months. When you take it out and try to chew it and it gets stuck in your teeth, you wonder how things have fallen so far apart. You really should have let it be, you greedy summagoat.[2]

Some stereotypes are actual factuals, and the one about Nigerians not being on time for anything is one I won't even debate. You might be thinking, "Hey, that's not fair. You should not attribute certain behavior to an entire group of people!" You're right. I shouldn't. But I'm going to, because this is my book and I do what I want. Find me someone who is Nigerian who is always on time for things that aren't work-related and I will find you a Tyrese quote that makes perfect sense. They might exist, but they sure are rare.

Just beware. If you're hosting an event and you invite Nigerians, don't be surprised when we show up as everyone else is leaving. We'll stroll in three hours after the start time wondering why the lights are up. We'll be upset that no one got to see our cute outfits and you have no food left—you have some nerve not saving any for us. We even spent thirty minutes looking for that errant lid for the Tupperware we brought. Ugh. Selfish.

If you want us to be on time for anything, we have to be tricked into it. Baby shower at 5:00 p.m.? Print special invitations for your Nigerian friends that say, "Shower starts promptly at 3:00 p.m." We'll probably get there around 5:45. Similarly, if a Nigerian event is slated to begin at a certain time, don't expect it to begin for at least two hours afterwards. If you show up at the time it is

---

[2]*summagoat*: Because sometimes folks act like they're the spawn of goats. Also, sometimes "son of a bitch" feels too harsh.

supposed to start, you will walk in and see the host in pajamas and the interior designers still setting up. You might be invited to help finish unfolding the chairs and putting the plates on the tables. Make yourself useful, bro.

True story: I once went to a Nigerian wedding that was supposed to start at noon. My family members and I showed up at 2:00 p.m. (because we cannot be helped), thinking we would have missed the church ceremony and be on time for the reception (hell yes, cake!). Well, imagine our surprise when we walked into the church and everyone was sitting there waiting and no one was at the altar yet. Long story short, the wedding did not start until 3:30.

It's a vicious cycle of tardiness. Since you know that *everyone* will be late for a Naija event, even if you were planning to be on time, you don't want to be the only person there. So you sit at home on your couch fully dressed and opt to go late so you won't be the first person to arrive. And when you show up three hours late and you're one of only five people there, you remind yourself to arrive even later next time.

There is nothing that I've ever not been late for. I'm the person who shows up to the airport thirty minutes before my flight is supposed to leave, and ends up running through security like a madwoman. One time, I showed up as boarding started and heard my name being called over the intercom. I got through security, threw on my boots without tying them, and ran with all my might. I got about ten feet before I tripped on my laces and face-planted in the middle of O'Hare Airport in what felt like slow motion. I broke my shoelaces, and my dignity got drop-kicked through the goalposts of life. I made the flight, though! The lesson I learned from that experience wasn't to be more punctual; it was "Don't wear shoes with laces when you're flying." It's so bad that my friends now call running late for a flight "the Luvvie."

Clearly, shame be mad busy in my life. I have earned all the judgment. Now that it's in print, I have permanent proof that I should be ashamed of myself.

You know who else needs to be ashamed of themselves? Dinner scrooges.

Is there an event more painful than a group dinner where more than five people are present? Being in the club is no longer my cup of tea. Now, my idea of fun is a night at home on the couch binge-watching my bae, Netflix, while rocking the ugliest but most comfortable pajamas I can find (the fuzzier, the better). This is a standing date, and it must begin by 10:00 p.m. at the latest. I can let many people down, but not Netflix. We have a love thing.

So when it's someone's birthday, the most I can handle is usually dinner. Brunch is a close second because booze in the daytime seems to taste better. Plus, we're allowed to loiter in one place for a while. WIN.

The great thing about dinner is that you get to see the folks you've been promising to go out to lunch/coffee/drinks with all at once. The bad thing is that someone or multiple people will walk away pissed off. Why? Because of the inconsiderate beings who walk amongst us. I call them "dinner scrooges," because there's always a problem with them when it's time to open the wallet.

I hope you're not one of them, because someone ought to kick you in the shins if you are. There are three types of dinner scrooges:

Dinner Scrooge #1:
The person who eats a lot and wants to split the bill equally

It's time to order, and most people will get an appetizer, an entrée, and a drink. But you get to Dinner Scrooge #1 and he orders three of everything. He needs that crab rangoon, the shrimp shumai, AND the cucumber salad. He couldn't pick just one starter. Then he gets the pad thai, the spicy basil leaves, and the curry noodles.

Whatever, no one cares. He also wants the Thai iced tea and two strawberry mai tais. At this point, I'm pitying his porcelain throne and what he will do to it later, but YOLO and all that jazz.

We all eat, drink, and merry the heck outta the evening, and then the bill comes. Dinner Scrooge #1 is the first person to recommend that we all split the bill equally to make life easier . . . on everyone.

The devil is a LIAR and a CHEAT and the truth ain't in him. No, sir! No, ma'am! No, Bob. What you're *not* gonna do is order the entire menu, order off the secret menu, and get some to take home so you won't have to cook through the week and then want everyone to subsidize your bill. All I got was that wilted kale salad that tasted like the tears of my disappointed ancestors and water with a lemon wedge that was probably dropped on the floor before it made it into the glass. I am not putting down $65.39 just because you wanted to let your inner glutton shine on that night. Nope! The fact that Dinner Scrooge #1 even fixed his mouth to suggest it makes you side-eye him, because this was his plan all along.

So he drops this "idea," and it gets quiet while everyone does calculations in their heads and notices that the only person with a take-home bag is Let's Split It Lonnie (aka Dinner Scrooge #1), and he's also kinda drunk, so there's proof that he had his fair share of alcohol. No one wants to be "that person" who calls out the bullshit, but I usually volunteer as tribute and bring up the unfairness and everyone else breathes a sigh of relief. If we had all ordered one of everything, it would make sense to split the bill equally. But you picked tonight to eat and drink your feelings on our dime, and we ain't having it. What we *will* do is break out these calculators and figure out roughly what everyone owes.

Anywho, have a seat! Wait, you're already sitting down. Stand up and then sit down again just for the purpose of reassessing yourself, your suspicious math, and how you treat your friends.

Dinner Scrooge #2:
The person who calculates their
bill to the cent

Sometimes it really is easier to split the bill and have everyone pay the same amount. *Sometimes.* The only time it works is when everyone eats comparable meals and everyone at the table is actually friends. (*See* Dinner Scrooge #1.)

Instead, there's usually that one person who insists that they had *just so much less* than everyone else, even when it's not true. The bill comes and they break out the phone and their restaurant-bill app and they calculate their food cost down to the cent. Somehow this person also manages to have change in their wallet. Who is carrying around thirty-seven cents exactly?! Are you someone's Grandma Beulah? Is that a two-dollar bill in your wallet? Who are you, and why are we friends?

Dinner Scrooge #2 puts down their exact change, looking smug that they've come prepared—Cheapskate Charlie face. And you know they always forget to include tax and tip. Unacceptable.

Dinner Scrooge #3:
The person who leaves early
and forgets to pay

Everyone is breaking bread and having a great time when that one person who is always busy says they must leave early. Oftentimes, I'm that person. Let me take this time to confess that it isn't always because I have something to do. I just don't feel like talking anymore and I'm one hour overdue for my personal Netflix marathon and fuzzy pajama time.

The early leaver grabs their coat, and in the midst of the good time everyone waves them off and gives air hugs and kisses. But when the bill comes, we all realize that Dinner Scrooge #3 forgot to pay their portion before bouncing. Okay, it's possible for this to happen once because we're all entitled to occasional absent-mindedness. Or maybe they are going through a rough time and are embarrassed—which is bad, but forgivable if it doesn't happen allatahm.[3] But when this happens twice or three times with the same person, you realize that you are being duped and they can't be invited to group dinners anymore. They totally can't sit with us any longer.

I wish they would just be open and honest and let us know if they're going through a down time or a broke period. One of us can totally cover their meal, but they never let us know so we can temper our expectations.

I have to say, group dinners really can be painful. Even when no one is being shady with money, there always seems to be a shortage of it once the bill arrives. Either none of us can count, or . . . yeah, I'm actually pretty sure that's a possibility. Math is hard.

* * *

In fact, don't invite me to a group dinner unless everyone has been told to bring cash, or there's a fixed menu. Or you know for a fact that I can get my own check, because I do not have time to spend two and a half hours eating a really fancy, bland dinner and then another hour trying to figure out the payment situation. I have a life to live, and I don't want to have to ask my eyebrow lady to come meet me at this restaurant because I've been there for three weeks trying to reconcile the maths. Thanks for understanding.

The only way a group dinner can be worse is if there are toddlers present. Let's be honest, toddlers are the worst. Those tiny humans are needy and they want your constant attention and then they need your help doing everything. *They are so lazy.* Then they have the nerve to cry and throw tantrums and be ungrateful. And

---

[3]*allatahm*: "All the time" just doesn't have the same ring to it.

you just want to ask them, "What have you done for *me* lately?" You don't want to negotiate with tiny terrorists, but you're in Target and they wanted that ball really bad and you don't want them to fall out in aisle 20 and make everyone look at you funny, so they win. Those mini-villains win every single time.

I am not immune.

One time I went shopping with my niece and she was such an angel in the car. She sang, she clapped, she made my ovaries do the wop because she was perfect. Then we stepped into the store and it was like she got possessed by an evil spirit of bad behavior. I got her into the cart and was weaving through the aisles, giddy about being in my Happy Place. I turned around to get something off the shelf—my back was only to her for twenty seconds tops, *tops*—and when I went to put my goodies into the cart, she was standing up in it.

How the hell did she do that so fast? She let herself out the seatbelt and somehow jumped up quick enough to be standing there looking like she just discovered America. She was so proud of herself, and there I was, slack-jawed. I plopped her right back down and buckled her seatbelt. Then I got real close to her face and whispered through gritted teeth, "You. Stay. Seated. Or. We. Will. Have. A. Major. Problem."

She looked frightened by this and chilled out. I was proud and thought to myself, *I'm going to be an awesome mom, because I've already mastered the art of threats that are so palpable that you don't even need to speak them above whispers.* But ten minutes later when we passed a toy aisle she spotted an Elmo doll, and it seemed like the store went silent right before she screamed, "I WANT ELMO! I WANT ELMO!" *Y'all.* Why must you show out like this in front of people, Little Jerk?

Toddlers are couthless. LORD. They are so couth-deficient. They'll tell you "those shoes look like my nightmares" without a second thought because your feelings don't matter to them. Yes, they might save you from embarrassing yourself when you go out in public by pointing out that you look like the radioactive stick they saw on their favorite TV show. But *still*. Toddlers are just short, mean teenagers. The only real difference is that toddlers are still cute, so we can deal with them better. That cuteness is the reason we get all attached to them in spite of their shenanigans, so by the time they grow up, we feel all responsible for them and whatnot. It's really a conspiracy.

Between our perpetual lateness, our failing at dinner parties, and the tiny tyrants we allow to boss us around, we are the worst, and I'm judging us all.

Why Must You Suck at Friendship?

 Friends are the bonus gifts of life because they are the people who are closest to us who aren't really required to be there. They're not bound by blood, and they won't be at the family reunion, so you can drop them if you need to with no problem. Unless you're roommates, in which case you're bound by a lease, and did they really have to GChat you to tell you the rent is due like you haven't been on time every month? I mean, that's just ridiculous. Ugh.

Good friends are often our lifelines. Mine have seen me through heartbreak, through the deaths of loved ones, and through that phase in college when I was obsessed with denim jumpsuits and matching fingerless gloves. They stayed by my side in spite of the fact that I chose to look like bad decisions and Levi's factory remnants. For this, I am forever indebted to my BFFs. But just as there are those amazing compadres who make our lives better with their presence, there are also those who might be bringing down our property value.

Friendship is a two-way street, and some people block the way like a parked U-Haul truck in the middle of your road of friendship so school busses can't get past, and that's just rude. Although life doesn't have actual violation tickets, some people should get the boot. Some folks don't deserve nice things, like matching "Friends Forever" bracelets.

I am judging those of us who are these friends:

The friend who competes with me (The Competitor)

It is said that we are the sum of the five people we hang out with the most. This means we should draw inspiration from our closest friends, seeing their growth and triumphs as a push to be better ourselves. But then there's the friend who I like to call The Competitor. This is a person who feels like their life is in direct competition with others', and any win for someone else means they must trump it. Do not be this friend, because we're not all in the same race, so why do you think we're in the same lane?

It happens like this: Something fantastic happens, and you pick up the phone to tell The Competitor. They applaud you momentarily and then they remind you of something they did that was similar, but at a higher level. Every single time. They're so used to doing it that they don't even realize it, and you start telling them your good news less and less.

If you tell them that you just got a new job, they'll tell you they've been promoted to Topflight Job Haver of the World. If you say that you got an A on your paper, they'll retort that their paper was considered the best in the class. Their superpower is being able to make any good news you have into something about them, and you will eventually realize that they really do not wish you well. Your joy is an ever-present reminder of their failures, and nobody needs that in their life.

The Competitor will get engaged at your wedding, just so the spotlight can be on them. Then you'll have to have your baby at their reception as they cut their cake, to return the favor. You will get afterbirth all over the UGLASS[4] neon tulle bridesmaid dress they made you wear because they didn't want you to outshine them. It's the Circle of Life of Pettiness.

The friend who only calls when they need something (The SOS Pal)

We all go through tough times where everything sucks and we just need to lay our burdens on the ears and shoulders of our friends. Needing support during hard times is a part of life, and our friendship villages exist partly so they can hold us up when we're weak. When times are better for us, we in turn reciprocate that love and support. However, there are some friends who are only around when *they* are in need. They take, but when it's time to give they're missing in action, like the edges of someone whose braids have been too tight for ten years. I like to call these friends SOS Pals. I am judging people who allow themselves to be SOS Pals so often it becomes a part of their character.

SOS Pals will call you whenever they're in crisis mode and need help. You might have to loan them money, bail them out of jail, or act as their alibi when they've been doing something they weren't supposed to. They're broke; you get a call. They need a job; your inbox blows up. They're sad that day; you get a sad emoji in your texts. You've put on your therapist/caretaker suit for them, and now you are the Batman to their Gotham. This is co-dependence and it can become unhealthy, especially when your relationship with this friend is reliant on you always playing Captain Save-a-Pal.

You do it because this is what friends are for, not because you're expecting some medal of honor. However, this principle falls to pieces when you do not hear from SOS Pal when things are on the

---

[4] *UGLASS:* Gives "UGLY ASS" some weight.

upswing for them. In bad times, you're in their phone's "Favorites" list, but in good times, you only find out what they're up to via social media along with everyone else. You go from bestie to follower quick, finding out that they're now engaged or they got that promotion at the same time as their seventh-grade classmate who they just friended on Facebook the week before, when normally they're taking the "call me anytime you need" mantra literally with 3:00 a.m. sobbing conversations. They know your number when they have a dilemma but forget it for celebrations.

SOS Pal also does not call you to check up on you, and there have been times when they called you in their emergency and you mentioned yours, but they brushed it aside, because "this is about *my* pain." You end up feeling taken advantage of because your friendship is truly one-sided.

When I was in college, my BFF was the de facto therapist of our dorm floor. People would go to her room at all hours to vent and cry and whine and throw tantrums. She was an always-present listening ear who was wise beyond her twenty-year-old self. *Everyone* was an SOS Pal to her, because none of us seemed to realize she was going through her own struggles and heartbreak. Then one day she left a note on the dry-erase board on her door: "I've run away. Wipe your own asses from now on. —Management."

Touché. Tou all the chés.

We have all been SOS Pals at some point in our lives. But when we are out of our crisis beds, we need to make an effort to also be there for those who we just used as pillows. Don't drop your burdens on people without also being willing to drop some blessings on them, too. They are not your dumping ground for life's problems.

How do you know if you're an SOS Pal? Look at the last texts or calls or e-mails you've sent to your good friends. Have they been all about you for some time? Then yes, you are one. Call your friends up and ask how *they're* doing.

The friend who will one day get us beat up or arrested (The Adventurer)

There are some friends who push us out of our comfort zones, and The Adventurer (aka Reckless Robin) is that type of friend. They live life on the edge, and sometimes it gets them into messy situations. They act like rock stars, but without the fame and money.

The Adventurer is captain of Team No Chill because they love being spontaneous in every way. They can turn a simple brunch into an event worth telling a story about later. You love them for keeping you on your toes, but you kinda fear for your safety when you're with them. Going out with them is like going on the Oregon Trail: you might end up having an exciting adventure or you might end up with dysentery. They really do epitomize "Turn Up" and "Rules Are Made to Be Broken." They are basically that friend your parents warned you about.

The Adventurer enjoys drama. You're probably afraid to travel with them—what if you end up in jail on another continent because they convinced you to visit that museum after it closed? I lack survival skills, and I don't need my life to resemble a sequel to *The Hangover*. Although my Adventurer friend can be a great time, like when she took me to get a tattoo in Miami at 1:00 a.m. (from Lil Wayne's artist), we got my friend's mini-Chihuahua drunk off two strawfuls of margarita at Wet Willie's, and then we slept by a pool at a random hotel until morning. Then we got our luggage and went straight to the airport, smelling and looking like last night's bad (but fun) decisions. Good times.

Adventurer friends are down for anything, and sometimes that means they're also down to fight. You're afraid to go out with them because they might say something that somebody will take the wrong way, and then you might find yourself having to defend them. You realize that even though you know how to talk mad shit, when it comes down to the actual execution of a proper fight, you are ill equipped. You'd both get your asses beat if a Jets versus Sharks situation were to go down. You have to hope it never comes to that and that you can instead just circle each other and settle it with a Running Man competition.

Still, everyone needs at least one person in their squad to keep life interesting and to be in charge of their bachelor/bachelorette party, even if you'll end up late to the altar, hungover and wondering if you broke some vows before even reciting them.

If you're this friend, I'm not really judging you as much as envying you. You have way better stories than I do. Also, no, I do not want to come to Antarctica to float on a glacier for three days. I'll be looking forward to your pics, though! Send me a postcard.

The friend you don't/can't trust (The Lannister)

There are some people who we feel we are obligated to remain friends with because of either proximity or history. Maybe you were born at the same hospital on the same day, and your moms are BFFs because of it. Or maybe you have so many friends in common there's no way you won't have to see or hang out with this person. You might really enjoy their company because they're fun to be around. Unfortunately, you know you can't trust them. They have done things in the past to others around you, and you can tell that they could easily do the same to you. Like the time they slept with your other friend's boo. Or when they stole from someone and got caught. Maybe they did something traitorous and later apologized, but there are some things you cannot come back from. Again, they might have done nothing to you personally, but like Mother Maya Angelou says, "When people show you who they are, believe them."

So you know The Lannister is not to be truly trusted. You would not leave them alone in your house, and they surely cannot stay overnight. You don't mind inviting them to brunch, but you have to compartmentalize the friendship. Keeping them at arm's length is your best bet, and a way to keep them from infiltrating your life with foolishness. College was full of these friends, but you managed to drop many of them after the pomp and circumstance of graduation.

This type of person will stab you in the back, and then they'll use that same knife to butter their bread at your group brunch the next week. Basically, they're a Lannister from *Game of Thrones*. You might not like hanging out with them, but it's safer to be able to keep an eye on them. Keep your friends close and your enemies closer.

The friend who you don't really know (The Surface)

We all have that mysterious friend who we've known for years and years. We might have gone to elementary school, high school, *and* college with them. They are part of so many of our memories that they are more than just acquaintances. However, you don't really know them beyond the surface level because they are very guarded with everything. They take real Gs moving in silence like gnomes to new heights. Are they in a relationship? You have no idea. What is their pet's name? When did they get a pet, anyway? What kind of job do they have? You're not sure. Are they in the CIA?!

I feel like everyone knows this friend, a Tommy from the TV show *Martin*. I like to know what the people in my life do for a living. Does that make me nosy? If so, I'm okay with it. I just enjoy knowing that everyone in my circle is gainfully employed and prospering at whatever occupation they've chosen. And unless being forever unemployed is your stated life choice, I expect to know something about how you make your livelihood.

One of the things we all assume is that to function as an adult you have to make money, and to do that you have to get a job. Unless you're a trust-fund baby. But one day, we realize that one (or a couple) of our friends seemingly have jobs, and yet no one knows what they do. We try our best to get clues from them, and they never give us a straight answer. We even ask if they're on

LinkedIn (because at least that will tell us) and when we finally find them, the only info on their profile is the college they went to. (I see what you did there—you've won this round.) Their major isn't listed, or it's something like "Liberal Studies." If y'all went to college together, you don't remember them even being at graduation, because they probably skipped the ceremony to go to some concert. Maybe you saw their degree once in a Facebook picture, but only their name was visible. So at least they're post-bac.

When you realize that Google isn't turning up anything useful either, you decide to ask them outright. "WHAT. DO. YOU. DO?" Then they act like telling you would put the republic's security in jeopardy, giving a completely vague answer that leaves you even more confused than you were to begin with. Sir, are you a member of B613? Are you a secret operative on an undercover mission to make us all question your ability to hold down a job? What is the big deal?

Look here, Tommy. You with your clear business card and your office in the building with no windows: I hope what you're doing isn't illegal. In fact, maybe it's best you *don't* tell me. If I get a random subpoena one day with your name on it, it's best that when I say "I don't know," I'm not lying. I should probably stay in the dark.

With The Surface, you just come to accept that you will never know what they do or too much about their life at all. You love them anyway, even though every time they start talmbout[5] their rough day at work all vaguely, you wanna yell "WHAT IS IT THAT YOU DO, TOMMY?!" But again, you've reached acceptance. They're still the homie. But . . . side-eye.

The friend who is mean (The Frenemy)

Some "friends" make you wonder why you have enemies, because they are literal mean girls or boys. They've made it their job and

---

[5] *talmbout*: Because "talking about" is too many syllables sometimes.

their life's purpose to use you or someone else in your group as a verbal punching bag. They might try to disguise it with backhanded compliments, but their true colors shine through. They're good for uttering statements like "Let's go out to eat tomorrow. I know you don't go to the gym now," as they look you up and down. They throw so much shade that you have to use your flashlight app when you're around them. The worst part is that because they know your insecurities, they're adept at picking at your emotional scabs.

Why are you still friends? Probably because they weren't always like this, and the good memories from your long friendship prevent you from dropping them like a bad habit. However, at this point they are one more comment away from you kicking them in the ankles. Maybe life is rough for them right now, but they don't have the right to be such buttwipes. Actually, drop them. Maybe when they learn to be nicer people you can be friends again. Or not.

The friend who yeses you to death (The Enabler)

Friendship isn't about having the exact same opinion all the time, or never having an argument. Friends should also be able to tell us tough truths and help correct things we do that aren't on point. This is why the friend who cheers on every single thing you do is not the best. They never challenge you, even when something you do is obviously wrong. Take them shopping and they will convince you that everything you pick up will look amazing on you. You test them by picking out some jersey culottes, and they swoon. This is how you know they cannot be taken at their word. Culottes look good on nobody, and when they're jersey knit, the number of wedgies one will get throughout the day is unforgivable. Friends don't let friends wear jersey culottes unironically.

Your enabling friend is a sweetheart, and the opposite of a mean girl. You just wish they'd have a differing opinion once in a blue moon. But you enjoy the fact that you can go to them and get a high five for even the dumbest things you do.

The friend who is undependable (The Flake)

Then there's that person we all know and love who is as unreliable as a meteorologist in Chicago. You live in the same city as them, but you only see them once a year. Why? Because their superpower is that they will find a way to flake out of any and every event. How do you catch a cloud and pin it down? You cannot. Flaky friends just cannot help themselves. They love making plans, but the day or the night before, they send you a text with some vague excuse as to why they cannot make it. That's actually them being *good* with follow-through, because sometimes they cancel at the time you were supposed to meet. You're sitting at the table next to the window when you get a text from them about how they got stuck in the suburbs, and you shake your fist because you should have known better. The worst is when they "forget" you even have plans at all, and you wait for an hour before hitting them up and get the "OMG WAS THAT TODAY?" routine. Dambit!

The Flake is just so undependable, and it's a lesson you will learn over and over again. You love them dearly, but if you're ever on fire, they will say they'll put you out and then show up without a bucket of water because they forgot their neighbor borrowed it. Come on! You had one job. ONE. JOB. Ugh.

This friend is good for one thing: when you want to have a reason *not* to go somewhere. Use them as an excuse and no one who knows them will think to blame you. "Aw, man! I really wanted to go, but I made plans with The Flake, and then she canceled at the last minute. So unfortunate." *Sips wine*

The friend who disapproves (The Holy Roller)

I love Jesus as much as the next person, but some friends are hard to be around when they're all Jesus, allatahm. Of course there's nothing wrong with taking pride in your spiritual beliefs, but they take it overboard, and it makes them hard to talk to. You have to second-guess your decision to invite them to a girls' night in because you know you're all going to start talking about sex, and that makes them uncomfortable.

Can grown people please have healthy conversations about who we decided to do the horizontal tango with without the judgy eyes? "Ohmygoodness," the Holy Roller will gasp, "you slept with him and you've only known him for a year?" The worst part is when you remember how free they were before they got born again. You don't want to point out their hypocrisy, because the high horse they're sitting on looks comfortable, but you're tempted.

You can't tell them anything you're doing if it isn't sanctified and holy. You can only talk about so much, so they're the friend you tell when you finally go to church on Easter. And then they're proud and think their efforts at converting you are finally working. And you can't tell them that the only reason you went is because you knew Mom would side-eye you if you didn't.

✳ ✳ ✳

At one point or another, we've all been one of these bad friends, even if just for a spurt of time. The key is to not embody these traits. We shouldn't make a habit of being the anti–Golden Girl. (Although you know Blanche Devereaux would totally sleep with your husband. Probably on your wedding night, too.)

When Baehood Goes Bad

Love is blind and can render you averse to making sensible decisions. Sometimes, we get into relationships and lose all semblance of grounding because those endorphins have us all googly-eyed. This is why I must judge us for baehood that goes bad.

My friend was dating a dude who defied logic by being about twenty types of terrible. I was actually impressed by his inability to be a well-functioning adult. It was like he was allergic to adulting. But I'm thankful for him because he is proof positive that I need to get my creativity game up, because I could not make up a better story of when baehood goes bad.

We will call my friend "Tina," and we'll call bad bae "Carlos." Tina is a professional lady with a job that has benefits and perks and a good salary. She owns her own apartment and she enjoys long strokes in the sheets. Carlos was a dude with a bike. That's about it. As in, Carlos's bike was the most valuable possession he had, and it was his only mode of transportation. His employment was questionable; Tina didn't know what he did, and I suspect she was afraid to ask. It would be nice to assume that he worked at the casino, since he spent so much time there. Carlos clearly had a bit of a gambling problem, because only people who are paid to work at the casino should be there so damb much, especially when it's fifteen miles from your house and you have to ride a bike all the way there every day. GO HOME, ROGER.

Anyway, Tina was filled with Carlos-lust, and he was best when he was horizontal (well, sometimes vertical, because he did that trick where he held her up and . . . lemme stop). How do I know all this? Because one night when she was frustrated about him she spilled the beans. It was raining outside, and he was at the casino, unable to get home because his bicycle was a bicycle and not a damb car. He wanted her to come pick him up and had the nerve to get mad that she was not about that life.

I was like, "Let me make sure I get this straight. Your boo, who is a gambling addict riding around town on a bike, got mad at *you* for not wanting to scoop his ass up because it was raining and he was stuck at the casino?"

She huffed, "Basically," and I realized that I need friends with higher self-esteem and better decision-making skills, because Jesus be some discernment to pick them better. Also, was Uber unavailable on that rainy night? Did public transportation go on strike? How do you get stranded at the gahtdamb casino, Jobless Jonah?

Anywho, she didn't pick him up and she didn't hear from him for another week, and he was not returning her calls. Was Bicycle Bob *that* mad that she didn't give him a ride? She was worried about him, so she decided to go check on him at his mom's house. Because that's where he lived. Let me repeat that. Tina went to Carlos's mama's house, where he lived, to find out why he was not returning her calls. When I tell you I was so done that I was burned to a crisp on the inside? I went from medium rare to burnt so quick. *YOUR TEN-SPEED-RIDING, GAMBLING-ADDICT BOO*

WITH A TEMPER ALSO LIVES WITH HIS MAMA?!* In that moment, I wondered why my friend didn't seem to have mentors or role models or sense, because ain't no way this should be the chump she's dealing with. *No way.* I also wondered where I had gone wrong with friends so foolish.

But I needed to know what she encountered at Mom's crib. What happened?

Well, Ten-Speed Thomas's mom informed Tina that her son, the degenerate, was in jail. At least he wasn't just ignoring her. (Silver linings!) Why was he locked up? He had violated his probation, which she did not even know he was on. And why was he on probation? For making counterfeit money, which he used at the casino to gamble. He was back in jail for doing it again, because clearly he is dumber than a box of toenail clippings. This is NOT a situation where you ought to be too legit to quit, Bike Billy!

At this point, I wanted to write out all the foolishness on a giant whiteboard for her: "Gambling addict. On a bike. Lives with his mama. Expects you to pick him up when it rains. Goes MIA. Is actually in jail for trying to feed said gambling addiction." Clearly he isn't even any good at the gambling thing, because if he was winning, he wouldn't have to print fake money. And he would not be riding around town on a ten-speed, fifteen miles each way, to go get his money-flushing habit on. Carlos excelled only at failing perpetually.

THIS was the man she was now basically mourning, and I sat flabbergasted that she wasn't too embarrassed to tell anyone this. This is the kind of thing that you take to your grave and leave between you and your God, because you should be too ashamed. The sheer quantity of bad decisions here surpasses the number of snowflakes on Mount Everest. If I was with a nincompoop like Carlos, I'd deny it so hard that I'd get whiplash from shaking my head no so vigorously. He was a total IJOT,[6] and the story was so

---

[6]*ijot*: "Idiot," according to Nigerians when we insult someone with fervor.

entirely ridiculous that I wondered out loud, "How did you get here? Nobody's supposed to be here."

I didn't have to ask Tina why she was even entertaining Two-Wheel Tyler: that peen was TOO BOMB. Let me translate: Carlos was a dick deity. He was a penis prince. He was a stroke savant with a crowned cock, and my girl was a-dick-ted. (BA-DUM-TSS! I'm here all day, folks!)

There is a fact that cannot be denied or disproven by science. Lean in close and receive this truth: behind every ain't-good-for-nothing man are bedroom skills beyond measure. It's like the universe's way of balancing itself out. It should have its own chapter in every holy book and scientific text, because it is an actual factual.

So many of our worst heartbreaks were probably caused by men who wouldn't know responsible if it slapped them in the face. Sure, we should have realized they weren't about shit when the only texts we'd get were "What are you doing?" at midnight. But we remember the times we had in betwixt them sheets, and that one trick and how we needed a five-hour nap afterwards because they had temporarily stroked the spirit out of us and we needed to recharge. So I'm told by a friend, of course. I'm not saying I've experienced any of this. HEY, MOM! All of this is at play when we deal with men like Cycling Clyde. Tina was caught up in the rapture of Carlos's sheet skills. I almost understood. Although I still wouldn't have told a soul.

I think what happens is that these guys spend so much time working on being fantastic at sex that they have no time left to nurture and develop other areas of their lives. When you have perfected the art of making people orgasm at will with beguilements, shortcuts, twists of the tongue, and anglings of the body, then I get why you have no energy left for learning to read. I can see why you can't hold a job or file taxes. It's not your fault, gentlemen. You were so busy learning how to be of sexual service that you missed the class on being a decent human being. But none of us minded after we handed you the panny drawls and you proceeded to do the job so well that we wanted to tip you afterwards but we fell asleep directly. Reminisces about every Scorpio man I've ever dated. I can't even. MOM, SKIP THIS CHAPTER.

I've heard about Island Peen Syndrome, too. It's an urban legend (but proven true by Lauryn Hill's life) that sleeping with West Indian or island men will render you useless to functional life. Apparently, it is the kind of PINOT NOIR (shout-out to Tituss Burgess!) that will have you babysitting your enemy's kids willingly. Word on the street is that if you mess with the wrong (or right—OH SO RIGHT) sperm stick, you might find yourself washing dishes with a scarf on your head and no shoes on. Next thing you know, you've sold all your possessions and moved to a commune where you're Sister Wife #8. Endorphins are some intergalactic imbeciles. They tell us all lies sometimes. Things like "Exercise is fun" and "This guy is decent. Totally trust him."

This magic peen carrier is also the kind of man who will give you a promise ring—an entirely meaningless concept that perplexes me to no end—and not only will you accept, but you'll show it to all your friends and be so giddy that you miss all their strong side-eyes directed at you. And because he is perpetually "in between jobs" (code for "never working"), it's probably made of the finest in Diamonique stones and synthetic sterling silver. I don't understand them or their purpose. What are people promising when they exchange these rings? Is it one of those "I'm promising that one day I'll promise you my all" things? Are they a promise to one day get engaged? Because no one should be here for that promise inception. Are they a promise to get married? Because then they're engagement rings. See what I mean? Pointless!

If your insignificant other gives you a "promise ring," feel free to accidentally lose it down the drain. It has about as much importance and symbolism as a heart drawn in the sand at low tide. Who has time for these bald-headed can't-commit-to-real-things games? Promise rings are for eighth graders, not adults. A chastity promise ring? Maybe. A promise ring to stop smoking? I see it. A promise ring to one day propose to you like an adult? NO. The only folks who can get away with rocking promise rings should also have curfews. If you're grown as hell and you're walking around rocking a promise ring, you need to go sit down and think 'bout your life. I hate having a conversation with someone when they are wearing a ring on that ring finger, and it goes like this:

ME: "Aww, you got engaged? When?"

HER: "Gurl, nah. It's just a promise ring. Isn't my sweetie the best?"

ME: *Blinks slowly* *chuckles nervously* "Well, it was good seeing you."

If you're not ready to propose, get someone a pendant or a bracelet or a trip to Fiji. Don't be dangling what could be with a promise ring. And on the subject of stupid love decisions, someone who would accept a promise ring is also 98.2 percent more likely to get their partner's name tatted on them after their third date. It's science. Look it up. (But don't, because I made it up. It's true, though.) Tattooing the name of a significant other on you needs to come after careful deliberation, knowing that person for a long time, and taking a blood oath that forbids a breakup. It probably should not happen after that session where you had multiple toe twitches for the first time. You are not in your right mind, beloved.

Human beings are more shortsighted than bats in the daytime. Relationships start off all hot and heavy, and that honeymoon phase has us thinking new love is perfect love. This is certainly not the time to go to a tattoo parlor to get your beloved's name permanently affixed to your lower back. Or your bicep. Or your chest. Wait until you've woken up next to them in the morning and experienced their dragon breath. See if you're still 100 percent after the first couple of times their "Good morning" curled your eyelashes before they curled your toes. See if you still like them after you've seen their underwear in the middle of the floor even though the laundry basket is RIGHT THERE. Do you still like them after you meet their mother, who seems unwilling to let go of her "baby"? Do you still like them after you've had a major argument where you wanted to cuss out them *and* their ancestors? What about when they were sick and acting like they got polio even though it was just a cold? What about when they were down and out and lost a job? Are you still loving bae at their worst? If you haven't gone through any of this yet, methinks you should wait on the tattoos.

I am a believer that you don't know somebody until you've seen them handle conflict or seen them at their worst. If you love them through that, and you've considered it for a while, then maybe you can go get their name installed on your body. What *I* am not doing is getting permanent work on my body for temporary situations, like many relationships tend to be. I'm not getting nobody's name tattooed on me, not even my own. I'm not even sure I like *me* enough. I can prove my love is real in other ways. I can add you to my Hulu account and give you access to my Amazon Prime so you know what we have is legit. I might even share that last spoon of rice with you to let you really know that I'm here for YOU, boo. But tattoo your name on my body? NO SIR.

Part of me thinks people get tattoos of their partner's name to show that they're in it for the long run, on some ride-or-die type thing. The idea that folks need to stand by their boos in the face of any and all types of bad behavior and crap is nonsensical. It is something that gets many of us in situations that we feel guilty about backing out of because we feel like we need to be the Bonnie to their Clyde, even if we suffer tremendously for it. Like Tina and our boy Carlos. The moment Tina heard Carlos was in jail should have been the moment she bounced and considered that "relationship," which really was a fuckbuddyship, done. Odds were, homeboy was going to be doing the time he avoided the first time.

Now, you're probably saying I'm bogus or a flake. You're right. I am not ride-or-die. Those are some pretty limiting choices: So if I'm not riding, I gotta die? Can I get off and take the bus? Is "Let's talk about it" an option? What about "ride, or pause this if we need to"?

There are people whose partners have been sentenced to twenty years in jail and they're waiting for them. That is adorable and commendable. However, if you weren't with me shooting in the gym, or we weren't childhood sweethearts and BFFs, or I don't have your big-headed kids, I am certainly not gonna waste my best years as you sit in jail or engage in hijinks. Our love story will need to be paused until further notice. I am not doing a countdown for your freedom day, sitting by the gate for years. That's unfair. Shoot, I might be the mother of your kids, and if me "riding" ain't in the best interest of our spawns then I'm still getting off at the next stop and calling my friends to come pick me up. I'm "ride-or-surely-you-understand-why-I'm-done-here."

The way my loyalty is set up, you might get one Get Out of Jail Free card because we go together really tough and I love you, but what I will not be doing is enabling dysfunction by always being there when you royally mess up. Sorry not sorry. Don't be catching no cases on my dime. I got my Global Entry status and TSA PreCheck to protect. We are too grown for me to be constantly tied to your bad behavior. Who has time for that?

Far too many people allow this ride-or-die thing to keep them in expired relationships. If you constantly have to play ombudsman for your beloved, you're in a co-dependent prison of your own making. People will keep doing what they can get away with. When the relationship has soured, it should be like cutting off your mooching son's credit cards. Fly, little birdie! Get the hell out my nest!

To be ultrareal, ride-or-die expectations usually fall on the shoulders of women who often don't get the same level of commitment from their men. Men do not get told repeatedly to stand by their women no matter how much drama they bring into their lives. They get the message that they always have more choices. Meanwhile, women are told to stand beside and behind our partners in spite of their foolishness.

I can be loyal, but loyalty isn't blind commitment to cosigning on stupidity and bad decisions. Once my life starts being affected by your tomfoolery, I might have to moonwalk out. Some people have gone to jail for their boos, and I applaud them for their courage. That could not be me. If it comes down to me or you, *trust* I'm picking me. I can't fight, and my hair products are out here, so as you see, it would be harder for me inside. Thanks for understanding!

If we're both mature and grown, neither of us would want to put our partner in a situation that would put their livelihood and happiness in jeopardy. If you're constantly acting a fool, it means you aren't considering me in your actions, because clearly you don't care how they could affect your loved ones.

Call me simple, but I think baehood needs to come in less dramatic packages. My love motto is that my relationship should push me to be a better person. My partner should encourage me, challenge me, seduce me, and build me. I will aim to do the same. At any point in time, one person might be holding the other up, because isn't that part of being a team? You might have an off day, but your teammate picks up the slack. That's fine. There are times you'll both have an off day. Recalibrate and come back. Maybe the off day becomes an off week or off months. That's when you have to determine if you need to be on the same team at all.

If, of course, during the off week one of you goes and does something they weren't supposed to, like Ross did to Rachel, and a break baby happens, then all bets are off. Can we talk about break babies? OMG. Talk about true pettiness. You're having a rough time with your boo, so you go and have sex with someone else?

Petty. But a break baby means you went and had sex with some-one who is not your partner without taking proper safety precautions. *You didn't use a condom?* What in the hell is wrong with you?! I get that you might be distraught, but come on, bruh. Come on, sis. The *least* you can do is make sure you wrapped up. Not only are you being careless about yourself, you're also being careless with your partner's health. Break babies are beautiful. (Because all babies are beautiful. Even when they're funny looking, especially in those first few weeks when most of them look like baked potatoes—still beautiful human beings.) However, in the words of Dorothy Zbornak, the Sorceress of Shade, "CONDOMS, ROSE! CONDOMS!" Being on a temporary break doesn't mean you need to go dip your stick into anyone, or have your love pocket[7] dipped into with no protection.

Break babies are extreme, but baehood can go bad in much simpler ways. I've never been the type to check a significant other's phone or text messages or ask where they're going. I don't care where you're going, and I trust that you won't show up and act out. We've set certain boundaries and expectations in our relationship, and it is your prerogative to keep those in check. It is up to you to know what you can and cannot do. If you cannot tell me about it, then odds are you weren't supposed to do it and you feel guilty. That in itself is wrong. I did not attend any academies, so it is not my job to police you or try to catch you in any act. If I get to the point where I feel the need to do that, I'd just rather walk away, because it means you've lost my trust, and without that we have nothing left. Our foundation is cracked, and I'm not living in a shaky house. Leave if you can no longer be secure in what you've built. Fake forgiving-and-forgetting is pointless if you will always resent that person, or hold it over their head. I know myself. It's really hard for me to get over betrayals or lack of trust. Jesus for-

---

[7]*love pocket*: The word "vagina" just isn't romantic. I prefer "love pocket," because it is surely a pocket that is full of love and should be treated as such.

gives; I pout. This is why it's better for me to end things, because I will feel some type of way about you for a while. I would rather get that out of my system by myself than force a relationship to continue.

I do what's right for me, but of course after the breakup happens I'll be on my couch for weeks eating all the rice and ice cream and watching movies about why love sucks. I might even call you once to tell you how much you suck. But I cope.

You can do bad all by yourself, ladies and gentlepeople.

Under the Knife

You know how I know we've all crossed over the point of no return from doing the most with the absolute least? Anal bleach exists.

The day I saw an ad for anal bleach, I knew we had passed the point of no return, done a double backflip to the beginning, and run three more victory laps. We are at the point where we are so bent on perfection that we will lighten the inner sanctums of our assholes to achieve better beauty. The anus is the hole the body's garbage comes out of. We expect THAT to be pleasing to look at, too? I know for some it is a venue of pleasure (not that there's anything wrong with that), but *still*. Fascinating.

Can we stop? Can my prostate mouth be dark and brooding in peace? Why do we need our butt nostrils cosmetically whitened? Does my derriere tunnel really need to shine bright like a diamond? Come on, everybody. Do you do a photo shoot after the anal bleaching to show it off, or is this just for your own enjoyment? Like, when you're walking down the street, newly bottom-brightened, are you smiling to yourself with the satisfaction of your own personal "Let there be light"? *Maybe she's born with it. Maybe it's anal bleach!*

Gahtdambit, everyone. Why are we doing this? Who is this really for? People say "I did it for myself," but that's not correct. Unless you're really staring at your asshole in a mirror, day in and day out, disappointed that it has never reached its true fluorescent potential naturally, then that's not that accurate. When we die, will anyone exclaim over how light our anuses were in their rousing eulogies? Will the great loves of our lives remember fondly how pale our yansh-holes were?[8] Who gives a flying fuck? We're doing all of these things because we live in a world that has dropped a metric ton of pressure on us to be beautiful and made the definition of that beauty incredibly narrow and impressively unreachable. I am judging us for our shallowness, our impossible beauty standards, and our desperation to reach them.

Some people frown upon women using makeup to enhance their features and to feel more beautiful. I enjoy makeup as much as the next person, although I will say some of the ways we paint our faces gives me pause, like when we draw on our eyebrows and they end up looking like EKGs or other vital signs. But I don't think it's necessarily harmful. Here's what is: Do a Google Images search for the word "beauty." What comes up are pages and pages of pictures of white women. Even our number one search engine, no matter how algorithmic and formulaic its methods, equates beauty with lightness. If you yearn to be considered beautiful, wouldn't something like that lead you to think that to be beautiful you need to have less melanin in your skin? Around the globe, "White is right" is the message, and caste systems exist based on color; usually at the bottom of the ladder are Black and brown people. Folks face acute discrimination because of their darker

---

[8] *yansh* (also *nyash*): This is pidgin English (spoken in Nigeria) for "ass."

skin, and there's a major color complex that can be seen globally, across many cultures.

Centuries of hailing whiteness as the goal have gotten too many people believing that their dark skin nullifies their beauty. There are few things that make my heart as sad as the reminder that there are people in the world who are unhappy enough about their skin color that they'd cosmetically lighten themselves. Our skin is our natural coat and our largest organ. Our skin carries our history, whether white or Black or yellow. Our skin is part of our cultural heritage and is important in defining who we are.

Too many people believe that their dark skin voids their beauty. Some have been teased about their color by family, enough to where they start believing that something is wrong with the richness of their skin. The media thrusts those who are fair-skinned into the spotlight; even photography leans toward the preference of lighter-skinned people. All around us, the message is that the darker you are, the more inconvenient your beauty is. So I get how people could internalize all of that enough to where they artificially lighten their skin.

Skin lightening is a global issue, but I can only speak to my experience as a Nigerian. In Nigeria, bleaching is not uncommon. I do not want to speak out of turn in saying it has been normalized, but it sure feels like it. Folks refer to it as "toning" to make themselves feel better. Stores are littered with "toning creams" and ads with light, bright women, encouraging you to get your lightening on. Now, imagine that: a country where Black is the default, and yet people still feel pressure to lighten their skin. Even in a country full of Black people, we still cannot get away from colorism and the effects of our "white is right" ideas. Of course, there's the fact that Nigeria is a country that was colonized by the British until it gained independence in 1960. My mother was five years old when colonialism slinked back to Great Britain, but I have no doubt that its effects linger, and one of the ways they do is through the color complex the country is struggling with.

It is always jarring to see bleaching up close, no matter how common it is. People you've known your entire life but haven't seen in a year might show up looking like Casper the Friendly Ghost when they were previously the color of a Snickers bar, and no one can address the pink, bleached elephant in the room. We're all just supposed to carry on like you didn't run an eraser across your entire body. Meanwhile, I'm trying not to stare at your knuckles, which often refuse to take. It's like knuckles try to keep the hope alive, to remind you that you're lying like bad concrete. Knuckles are stubborn as hell. They are all about that telling-on-you life, and I appreciate it. The rest of you might be ivory, but those knuckles are a dead ebony giveaway.

You know I have no act-right and can't fix my face for a damb thing. Don't roll up to me without warning me that you became the Coke Zero version of yourself. Can I get a heads-up, so that when I see you I don't do a slow head tilt trying to figure out if I got cataracts, because surely this milky version of yourself must be an error in my visual field? Don't surprise me by showing up looking all Michael Ealy when you used to be the color of Forest Whitaker. Your feet will be on a mission to betray you, too, because they maintain their old color. They are also stubborn as hell, I've learned. When your face and your feet and hands look like they belong to different people, I know that Team Bad Decisions will never run out of members.

Gels and cream lighteners are often purchased off the shelf, or sometimes even mixed at home. Far too many people bleach without a dermatologist's assistance, so the opportunity for error is vast. Folks are outside with green undertones in their skin, green veins showing through, dark feet and knuckles, and a yellow face, looking like a walking Jamaican flag. It is such a mess. You did all that just so you could look like Joseph's Amazing Technicolor Dreamcoat, with skin of various shades, none that looks as good as your original one? Because when you decide to do this at home, without the care of a dermatologist, you *will* miss a spot. Or you'll get a bad formula and end up looking like a Dalmatian. People are out here looking like the Ghost of Fail Past, Present, *and* Future. Jesus be some protection against skin cancer, too, because chemical removal of melanin cannot be healthy in the long run.

Surely there's gotta be consequences to forcefully removing melanin from your skin with chemicals. I can only imagine that some of the folks who are doing this will end up looking like raw chicken in twenty to thirty years after their skin gives up on them from decades of lightening. Because bleaching your skin isn't something you do for one or two years and then stop. No. Melanin is resilient. It wants to come back and show out, so those who commit to being light against their natural complexion have to continue using creams to maintain the color. Melanin serves a purpose. It's nature's blessing and protection. It is natural SPF, and you're opting to remove it from your skin. Self-hate is a vainglorious vagabond, iSweaterGawd.[9]

The saddest part is that the shade of brown these folks were before was probably much better than whatever shade of light they're trying to go for. I'm saddened by the fucked-up pathology of inferiority that causes such desperation that people will do something so drastic. Why try to change who you were born to be and force yourself into who you think everyone will find more beautiful? Society has failed people to the point where they feel they cannot like themselves in the skin they were born in.

Whether it's our skin or the other parts of our bodies that we feel the need to change, we are doing our absolute utmost to attain perfection we can never reach. With our constant need to be beautiful, the message is that our original selves are never enough. If we're big, we want to be smaller. If we're small, we wish we were bigger. This has me concerned about our current state of affairs as citizens of Earth. I think we're officially taking our need for some narrow idea of beauty too far. Combining our global self-esteem

---

[9]*iSweaterGawd*: It's more polite than swearing to God.

issues with medical advancements, we are now at a point where plastic surgery has people doing themselves ultrawrong by having one, two, or twenty surgeries too many.

Now, don't get me wrong—I am not automatically against plastic surgery or other medical cosmetic enhancements. I admit that one day I might get tired of being the parliamentarian of the Itty Bitty Titty Committee. I bring the Doritos to our monthly meetings and sometimes I take notes, if I don't fall asleep during the introductions. I'm mostly there for the chips, though. Anywho, if that day comes, I might opt to upgrade these boobs from a size "404 Error: Not Found" to a C-cup or something; a proper one- to two-cup improvement, like the subtle lady that I am. I'm not ruling out Botox, either. If these laugh lines start looking like crop circles in my face, I might opt for something. Maybe, maybe not. Needles in my face do scare the shit outta me. I got a nose ring once and I cried for twenty minutes afterwards.

What I am against is cosmetic procedures (not medical necessities) that change what we look like to the point where we need new identification. That is what makes me frown. There are people who cannot even do Throwback Thursdays with the rest of us because they have brand-new faces and we'd all require receipts, two forms of ID, and their fingerprints. Why? Because they've opted to get facelifts, cheek implants, nose jobs, lip plumpers, chin shaves, and more. It is all too much.

And keep in mind that not all plastic surgeries/surgeons are created equal. If someone will be cutting into your body, you should probably do your research on them. They need to come with references, background checks, and word-of-mouth praise, and their office should have a four-leaf clover plucked from nature above the entrance. Any old doctor can't do it. This is not a thing where you want to go with the cheapest person you can find. This is not what you want to use Groupon to get a deal on. Go to the best of the best, so your face and body won't look like the universe is laughing at you afterwards.

After all, bad plastic surgery is like adding serious insult to injury. I've seen so many before-and-after shots where the "after" looked like a blooper reel. Every time that happens, an angel sings a sad song. People are out here shelling out thousands of dollars to be made to look like accidental cartoons. I've seen cheek implants that made someone look like Jafar from *Aladdin*. That surgeon was so damb petty. Boob jobs go awry far too often, too. I've seen some that look like two coconuts sitting next to each other, refusing to touch. Your implants should not look like they're giving each other the silent treatment. They really should communicate better.

And the people going from A-cups to GGG? First of all, *why*? That is a lot of boobage, and your chesticular region is gonna be all in shock. You go from ant bites to beach balls—OUCH. Why are you paying someone to give you shoulder and back pain? I will never understand that. Moderation does not need to take a nap when you're getting yourself cut up.

People are getting nose jobs that make their nostrils so small that they whistle when they inhale. Facelifts got their skin pulled so tight that it looks like it might hurt every time they have to blink, and their lips are so big and bloated that they look like they have a permanent allergic reaction to shellfish after a night at Red Lobster for an Endless Shrimp dinner.

To make matters worse, now teenagers are getting in on the action. Are their faces even fully developed? I'm pretty sure I made that up, but let's go with it. It's absurd to allow a fifteen-year-old to get cosmetic surgery. What do they know about true beauty at that age? At fifteen, I thought denim suits were high fashion. I knew nothing. I also thought I was a size nine shoe, when I'm really a seven. I can't even explain this. All I know is from my sophomore year of high school until college I bought size nine shoes and always wore thick socks. Then I got to college, tried on someone's size seven shoes, and realized they fit me *so* well! So everyone's shoes don't flop when they walk? I had been wearing the wrong size for three years; I was a dumbass. *That* person should certainly never have had the option to get plastic surgery.

Body dysmorphic disorder is a bombastic bastard. Surely it is to blame for some of these extreme surgeries people have. When they look at their reflection and see a funhouse-mirror version of themselves, of course they want to change it. *See*: Michael Jackson (may he rest peacefully) and Lil' Kim (who went from being a Black woman in 1995 to now resembling an Asian mermaid).

Just dambit. Dambit all. In the words of Queen RuPaul, "If you don't love yourself, how in the hell you gonna love somebody else?"

AMEN!

People who are girth-blessed get hell for it, but then folks go and objectify them for having ample yanshes. So now it's a thing, although Black people have had asses since forever. We (as a collective; not me) have been blessed with these bodies for centuries and we've been considered freaks for it (*see*: Saartjie Baartman). We've been ridiculed and made to feel like our bodies were somehow less than beautiful because we were pushing extra cushion. But then, one day, big booties started being celebrated in the mainstream. They became the new standard, and people started thinking they needed them to be beautiful.

Again with our ever-changing, impossible standards of beauty: we want women to have big boobs, small waists, and now, big asses. So now rates of butt surgeries and injections have skyrocketed. I reiterate: no Groupons for plastic surgery. Do your research!

Read this closely: if you insist on getting your ass by any means necessary, the least you can do is go to someone who is licensed. Google was invented so we can do better. Call the medical board if you have to so you can be super-sure that your doctor is authorized to do the work and not just someone who watched YouTube videos about giving butt injections. If your surgeon's office is someone's basement, it's probably not where you should be. Ask your surgeon for some receipts. If your surgeon also does hair in their office, that ain't who you want.

Do not be cheap about your procedures. This is not the place to skimp. Pay a premium, because your body is your house. *You need it to live.* Well, at least until we all have the ability to transfer our souls into robots when we ruin our bodies—but we're not there yet. For now, this is all you have. Yet people are dying from botched butt injections performed by fake surgeons and back-alley nurses without the certifications and degrees to do it. People are dying from allowing someone to inject unknown substances into their asses so they can be rotund. Again: women have actually *died* from quacks injecting concrete into their bodies. I am sad for everyone. Our common sense has officially jumped the shark.

If you die from getting your butt injection from someone raggedy and get to heaven, I hope the angels meet you at the gate and execute a choreographed group side-eye. You should have known better. I mean, big butts are not that serious. But if they are for you, get a personal trainer. Do squats, lunges, and all of that. If not, just accept your "flaws." Sure, your ass might be concave like a spoon. You might owe yansh. Maybe your back goes straight into your legs. So what? Develop an amazing personality so no one will care as much. Learn to make people laugh. Or just wear really big, distracting hats. There are things that will make your ass oweage no big deal. Look at me: I've just learned how to give side-eye so proper that people never notice my ass deficiency. What we lack in certain areas, we should make up for in others.

In fact, I realize that there are things about my body I could have decided to change but that have actually become reasons why I am who I am today. I also know that the LAWD is well aware of who He gives which gifts to. And this is why I do not have a ginormous yansh and am a semidecent person. I feel like the day the Lord was handing out booties, I was late (as usual) and so I missed out. Then, when I did show up to give an excuse, He took one look at me and said, "Nah, you look like you'd act a fool if I was to give you one of these," and He denied my application for a donk. He is indeed all-knowing.

I know for a fact that I would be awful if I was built like Serena Williams or Jennifer Lopez. I mean, seriously. Allow me to lovingly objectify those two ladies when I say "GOOD GAHTDAMB!" Those women are so beautiful; their bodies are the brick-house cherries on the sundae of life. *Whew.* If I had a body remotely close to what they have, I would be a terror. My ass would cause me to do really inappropriate and rude things. I'd be so ridiculous that people would be able to pick my labia out of a lineup. I'd wear zero clothes any- and everywhere, every day. I'd show up at church rocking a denim thong and a cropped T-shirt and have the nerve to sit right next to the head usher and dare her to say anything to me. And if anyone did say something to me, I'd tell them, "Jesus blessed me in many ways, and I am just showing off His works. HALLELUJAH."

People would be disgusted and appalled and I wouldn't care. All insults would just bounce off my ample backside. To whom much is given, much is required, and I'd require that my much would be given nary an inch of fabric. I'd hire a band whose sole job would be to follow me around and play theme music for my yansh, based on the mood I was in. They'd be called Ass Pandora. I might opt to walk backwards into any room I entered, because why not? I would be a good fool and wear short shorts in Chicago winters, because why should five feet of snow stop my show? I might also declare my booty its own limited liability corporation, assigning myself as CEO and chairman of the Donk. My jeans would be tax-deductible business expenses, and I would add my ass to my LinkedIn profile's Skills section. Everyone would throw hateration in my dancery, and I wouldn't even see it, protected as I would be by the throne I sat atop. I would just be up to all types of shenanigans. I'd be so stupid with it. I might tell people to refer to me as the queen of the Republic of Yanshmunda.

I would have no friends and no character. Thank goodness the Lord—who works in mysterious ways—gave me the petite body I have, because He knows how little behavior I'd have if He blessed me with a bodacious behind. Yes, I know I could go out and buy one of those bodies, but I'm glad that I'm built this way. It is part of what makes me who I am.

So to the Man Upstairs, thank You for doing the world a favor and not allowing me to have a ridiculous, tear-jerking, onion, dumbass, makes-no-sense booty. You truly are omnipotent and all-knowing, Father God. And to everyone who *is* built like a Coke bottle and still manages to have a conscience and be nice and put on clothes sometimes I say, kudos to you. You might not even have to read the rest of this book because clearly you're doing something right. This book wouldn't exist if I were you, because I'd be too busy being a menace to society. Because: shallow.

The moral of this story? Don't be the version of me I would be if I was gluteus maximus–blessed. Sure, rock makeup and hairhats[10] to your heart's desire, but don't die in the pursuit of different body parts, like giant boobs when yours were previously ant bites, or skin tone that started as Coke but ended up as Fanta. Yes, you can judge me because I just dedicated an entire half a chapter to talking about my yansh. But I'm judging YOU, I'm judging Lil' Kim's surgeons, and I'm judging society. Because everyone hates how they look, everyone wants what we don't have, and everyone is stuck in a cycle of so-called self-improvement that is really self-defeating. Do better, everyone.

---

[10]*hairhat*: Some wigs and weaves look like literal hats that folks placed on their heads. Therefore, they are hairhats.

Weight a Minute

One day, I was being interviewed for a feature story when the reporter made an offhand comment that he thought was a joke, saying "Aren't you like a hundred pounds?" He chuckled to himself, and I was stunned into silence. Sir, you got some ever-loving gahtdamb nerve. You don't know my life and yet you have the unmitigated gall to try to guess my weight. It wasn't even relevant to what the hell he was interviewing me about, and I was too flabbergasted to give a proper response. What did my weight have to do with the price of beans in Uganda? He felt so comfortable commenting on my weight, essentially making fun of my petiteness. I was pissed.

We suck so bad for shaming people's weight, whether heavy or thin. We talk about people's size constantly, and no one is considered perfect as they are. Folks are always trying to lose, gain, tone, or change their bodies in some way. We go in extra hard on big people. If you are deemed to be too girth-blessed, the vitriol that comes your way from all sides is outrageous, and it dwarfs any comments I've ever received about being small. I've witnessed a lot of fat-shaming, and I've probably been guilty of it, too, in the past. It's so commonplace and normalized that people do not consider how humiliating it can be to be ridiculed for existing in your natural body. This is why I'm judging us, for our collective contempt and shaming of people for their weight.

People have built entire comedy careers on making fun of well-built folks. Fat jokes are the discount-rack version of comedy, because everyone can get it but we all know it's not quality goods. They are not particularly clever and are never original. It is lazy, playground, low-hanging-fruit comedy, and folks trot it out when they're fresh out of other things to say. Basically, it means they should write better material, and shut the hell up until they do. When kids are making fun of their larger classmates, we can chalk it up to the foolishness of youth, but not so when grown-ass people do it. But here we are, a bunch of proud fat shamers.

At least some people know they're just being mean dust-canoes when they tell fat jokes. They have some semblance of self-awareness. If there's any credit to give them, here is the only place. Others, who are more insufferable, will claim that they joke about people who are plus-size to motivate them to have better lives. "I'm only making fun of them so they can lose weight and find love!"

First of all, nobody asked you to be Captain Save-a-Self-Esteem! What makes you think the person who happens to have more fluff needs your advice-by-criticism? If you want to do community service, find a soup kitchen instead of bullying burly people. No one believes you're that pressed about how healthy or unhealthy people are, either. You just want to get these jokes off to get cheap laughs. If someone is morbidly obese, I'm pretty sure that you insulting them is not going to be the catalyst for them losing weight. You're just adding to the world's negativity by being an inconsiderate asshat.

What the world needs now is love sweet love, not for people to further shame the plump about their bodies. They get more than enough messages telling them that they aren't beautiful or worthy of love or even worthy of being seen as humans deserving of dignity. Fat phobia is ingrained in every single thing we do or say around beauty and attractiveness. From our fashion industry to the media to children's toys, we are telling people every day that their allure as humans is based almost exclusively on the number on the scale, and it is damaging to our psyches.

Magazines and the fashion industry have been on the fat-shaming front lines for decades. All the models walking down the runways look like a strong gust of wind might render them past-tense. Why? They're wearing clothes that are supposed to be for women who buy clothes, not walking mannequins, so that just makes no sense to me. Being someone who is of a slender body type, these images do not make me want to purchase those clothes. But even as people publicly decry the obvious prejudice in fashion at every turn, it stands strong. It is as if fashion tastemakers are afraid that if women with bodies that aren't extremely thin show off their clothes, they might actually have to start making clothes that fit different body types. MON DIEU! Can you imagine?! What would people want next? Clothes in regular stores that go beyond a size eight? That would be too much to fathom! Let's totally ignore that the average woman is a size fourteen. But what is that, anyway? We wouldn't even know, because with the existence of vanity sizing, there are no standard sizes for clothes. Stores and designers are mis-sizing clothes, usually labeling them smaller than they really are, and everyone is spending money to be lied to.

As a slim woman, I get to take for granted the choices I have when shopping for clothes. For women who are plus-size, they either have to go to the few stores that cater only to them or they get the slim pickings in the tiny section hidden in the back of mainstream stores.

Would it kill labels and retailers to make clothes for women of all shapes and sizes? The afterthought of "curvy" collections at most retailers is insulting; the lines lack inspiration and fit. Style does not have to go on vacation just because designers need to use more material and a modicum of tailoring skill. Sheesh. They do these tiny capsule collections, and people have to celebrate these crumbs. The fact that it is worth celebration to even be thought of shows how overlooked they've been. And does the thought still count when it seems to come with minimal effort in execution? The lookbooks drop and people excitedly click just to find out that they're being offered glorified tents that cover them from neck to ankle. They're all like, "Here's a vaguely dress-shaped sack for you! Are you happy now?! Get off our backs!"

Celebrities who aren't skinny get treated like nuisances, too, dressed in glittery pillowcases for red-carpet appearances. Even the high-end luxury designers cannot seem to create styles that flatter larger women. It is not that these bodies are unable to rock clothes fiercely. They just aren't a consideration. It's unfair, it's harmful, and it needs to be fixed. Can my big-boned sisthrens live fabulously? Why is it so hard, fashion? It is because their beauty comes with an asterisk and is seen as an inconvenience.

I've witnessed firsthand some of our distorted perceptions of weight on red carpets I've been on. I've met many celebrities who are considered big—or, to use the code word, "curvy"—and I am here to say it's all hogwash and we are being lied to. Some of our favorite bootylicious icons are average-sized at best when you see them standing amongst people who don't make a living being judged for every extra ounce on their bodies. I saw a woman whose booty and shape is considered iconic and had to do a double take. I was expecting a Jessica Rabbit clone who was voluptuous and had ample everything. Her body was great, of course, but it was no bigger than a size four or six. That's right: your favorite "curvy" actress is probably a size four in real life, folks. Do not be fooled. It has to suck to be in an industry that is basically a funhouse-mirror land of what everyday people look like. Of course you seem fat at 140 pounds when everyone else weighs 105. It's an evil magic trick.

Male celebrities aren't as they appear, either. The ones you think are tall are five feet six inches on a good day and with their shoe lifts in. They've been standing around other short people so that you think because they have those guys beat by two inches, they're living tall. NOPE. The Hollywood house is nothing but four walls of distortion. Unfortunately, that fallacy compound is dictating to people what they should think about themselves, and that is problematic.

The TV and movie industries are certainly complicit in the incessant disparaging of my not-skinny boos. They have upheld the "fat isn't cute" crap for way too long, particularly against women. I notice that these standards do not apply as stringently to men, and that is an extra layer of bullshit in the GTFOH lasagna. Women's desirability is based on how small the number on the scale is. But men don't get the message that to be desirable or worthy of love they have to be in amazing shape, have awesome hair, and smell like roses even after a workout (and they don't even necessarily need to work out either). Onscreen, men can be burly and hairy and have no sense of style, but they will always snag the trophy girl (or boy). It's a tale as old as time and a formula as played as Yo-Yo Ma's cello.

We see this play out when chunky male characters who think they're Fabio are paired with hot wives who are dating way down, looks-wise. This is why Homer Simpson could pull Marge. It ain't like Homer had swag, either. He was a dimwit. Still, he snagged Marjorie.

Look across television for the last six decades and this type of physical pairing is evident in many portrayals of couples where the guy is big but his wife is skinny. *See: The Fresh Prince of Bel-Air, The Honeymooners, The Flintstones, The Simpsons, Married . . . with Children, The King of Queens*—ANY SITCOM. Literally just pick one randomly—you'll probably see it. We don't see the inverse too often. It goes too much against the grain to see a plus-size woman with a skinny or muscular dude. It ain't right.

In movies, you see the same dynamic: romantic comedies starring men who are not classically attractive, but the women they go after (and win) are usually stunning, svelte chicks. They check every box on the "You Must Have This Characteristic to Be Pretty" list, but they're with a dude who is average at best but happens to be smitten with them. The juxtaposition of a woman who is a total package still ending up with a partner who didn't even try, and looks like he might not have showered that day, is proof that we need to tell men they're cute less often. It is also proof of the unfair standards of beauty that women have to adhere to. Meanwhile, dudes just gotta show up.

Let's imagine, for a moment, a world where a plus-size woman carries a romantic comedy. Just think about that for a second.

Okay, moment's over.

You probably just thought about that longer than most Hollywood execs ever have. It's as if it is unthinkable that anyone would lust after a woman with extra meat on her bones. Let us completely ignore the fact that most of the adult population isn't under 120 pounds. If our entertainment is supposed to reflect our reality in some way, then Hollywood has created a bubble of distortion so airtight that it's spawned a new reality of its own. This Hollywood reality says stuff like, "Why would a love story be based around your plumpness? Why would men fall all over themselves? That's only for people who have thigh gaps! You will be the funny and goofy sidekick instead, because your beauty is better on the periphery. We wouldn't want to offend audiences by suggesting that plus-size women get courted and lusted over." We might have gotten *Bridget Jones's Diary*, but the premise of that movie was that the main character was big and messy but she was lusted after IN SPITE of her messy bigness. (And she wasn't even that big. I mean, *come on*.)

See what I mean? Bizarro World.

I'd love to see Melissa McCarthy cast in a role where a man professes his love for her and writes poems in her honor. Can we have that? Instead, she is always considered the underdog of love, or the person who presumably doesn't even need love because, since she's big, her snacks will keep her company at night. It's offensive.

No wonder eating disorders are out of control. People are seeing their weight represented as a liability and a hurdle to get past in order to be loved. Girls are growing up aware that their bodies are under constant scrutiny and feeling worthless because theirs don't come in Barbie's shape. No one's does, because they would have no room in their torsos for internal organs and their necks would not be able to support their heads. That nefarious programming starts early for us, though. Seeing yourself in the things around you sometimes helps you understand, even legitimize, your existence.

We are laughing and slandering something that a large (no pun intended) segment of the population is, and we gotta do better.

And while we ridicule people for being fat, we also turn around and say, "Real women have curves." Those curves, of course, are only valid as long as they don't go beyond some arbitrary point. That statement grinds my gears for many reasons. What about those of us who aren't curvy? Are the rest of us Pinocchio? I get the intent—to empower people who are bigger and frequently degraded—but it degrades others in order to do it. "Real women breathe." How about that? Don't tell me that because I'm shaped like a twelve-year-old prepubescent boy I'm not a real woman. Screw that.

It seems that we are never good enough. Everyone needs to be skinny, but not too skinny. You need to be thick, but not fat. We're pretty much the pits, and I can't help but judge us, because nothing weight-related comes with anything but scorn. Being skinny comes with its own problems. You might have just rolled your eyes at that. Well, shush. You will sit here and read about my struggles, because they are real. Of course the grass is always greener on the other side, but this is my book and I'll whine if I want to.

So, me. I've always been skinny. I've never weighed more than 120 pounds, and even that was probably with a bit of water retention. I totally celebrated not needing a belt that one time. Go, me! I've been the same size since high school, and if I still rocked Tommy Hilfiger like I owned shares in the company, I could still fit into all my old clothes. My metabolism is faster than Usain Bolt with the wind at his back, and no matter what I eat, I do not gain weight. Did you just rip this book up? STAHP! I mean it. These are struggles, for real.

When I hit puberty and everyone around me was sprouting boobs and ass, I barely needed a training bra. I remember one of my aunts walking up to me and pinching my nipples as a joke. Folks never shied away from telling me how skinny I was, as if it was brand-new information they just had to let me in on. I know I'm thin. You ain't gotta declare it like some PSA. I grew really self-conscious about my body and got a complex where I previously did not have one. What stuck with me, in particular, was how people focused on my skinny legs. I am basically Olive Oyl. My archnemeses are Timberland boots, because they're heavy and my skankles (skinny ankles) be on struggle mode when I rock them. I still do, though, because I'm shallow and I like the look. But good GAWDT. I wore them one day while in New York, and you know they walk *everywhere* there. These shoes are really not meant for those of us who are ankle-deficient, because by the end of walking those raggedy streets in some boy's size five wheat Timbs, and carrying that construction-boot weight with my ankles, I needed an Icy Hot patch. My lesson learned: wear thicker socks so your feet won't slide around in your cute boots. Also, ask a New Yorker for *exact* distance because they play too much. You ask how far y'all are walking, and they say, "Around the corner." Lies. I should have called Lyft.

I hated wearing shorts because of my aforementioned sticks for legs. In summer, I'd be in jeans the entire time—rain, sleet, 100 degrees, it didn't matter. At the beach, I'd wear long linen pants, and then when it was time to swim, I'd throw them off in a hurry and run into the water, all so people wouldn't see my legs and have the chance to point them out. And dresses? NEVER. Well, besides prom, and that was a gown so it covered my legs. It was a REAL insecurity. I carried this with me through my twenties, from which very few pictures of me in shorts exist. I don't know when I had my "I no longer give a damb" moment about my legs and my body, but one day, I put on a dress and looked amazing in it and decided that if people didn't like my toothpick legs, they'd just have to deal.

Anywho, for years, I did not like my body and was not comfortable in it because people constantly pointed out the fact that I was thin. What comes with being skinny is everyone treating you like you wrote in to their "Dear Abby" column. They're always ready to give you advice on what you need to do, even though you didn't ask them a damb thing. "Dang, Luvvie! You're so skinny! Do you eat?! Maybe you just need a sandwich." No, I don't eat. I survive on a steady diet of air and water. Don't worry about me, worry about you. You don't see me walking up to you, saying, "I see you've been eating. A LOT." Rude. It's mind-boggling how free people feel to do this to friends, family, and strangers alike.

Today, I recognize that my body type is idealized. In a battle of "Who gets it the worst?" I know to shut my mouth and listen and apologize for the dumb shit my fellow skinnies say. Some people are naturally meant to be fleshier, and some are like me and can't cuddle without stabbing their partners in the chest with their bony chins. It is out of most people's control. I have friends who weigh twice as much as me but eat half as much as I do and work out twice as hard. I'm pretty sure their hearts are in better shape than mine. They can probably run more than three blocks without wheezing, which is more than I can say for myself and my cardio abilities.

We're all walking around being told we're not enough, whether big or small, short or tall. It is exhausting, and we have got to be gentler with each other on this weight thing. It is ruining lives.

People are dwelling in hopelessness because their bodies are not whatever they're "supposed" to be.

I really do wish we could love ourselves more. It's something I am working on every single day. You're probably like, "Hey, Luvvie, don't you make fun of people all the time?" Yes, I do. As a professional make-fun-of-people-er, aka humorist, I excel at dirty dozens at others' expense. But I try my darndest to keep it to changeable things, like hair (come on, Jermaine Jackson. What *is* that on your scalp?), makeup (especially drawn-on eyebrows. Why do they look like windshield wipers?!), clothes (I see camel toe and moose knuckle. Do you have on underdrawls under those leggings? I'm asking for everyone), and fake teeth (you couldn't order the size small veneers? You had to go with the extra large? Oh, okay, then).

But we are more than the sum of our parts, and we are more than the numbers on our scales. Be like me and judge people by the decisions they make with their eyebrows. That's way more important.

Don't Be Pigpen

 I am not one of those people who is a neat freak. I am far from it far too often, because right now, odds are there's a pile of dirty laundry on my bedroom floor next to my hamper. I'm not sure why it will pain me so much to move the clothes over ten inches into their proper place, but here I am. I'm just really ready for science to come up with a robot that will do laundry for me, since this is the future and everything. It probably exists in Japan, since they already have robots with feelings. I'm frightened and impressed.

My point is, I am a lazy goat, so I am not saying everyone needs to live in a spotless house. However, I am here to side-eye those of us who allow our laziness to take over our lives and hygiene habits. Let it be noted that I am not talking about those people who are clinically depressed and can't get out of bed. You get my love and hugs from afar. Also, I am not talking about those who are homeless. Your situation makes me mad at all of us for failing to ensure you were never put in that position. And I am certainly not speaking about those who are disabled or medically unable. Nawl, not you. I exclude because I care.

Everyone else, though? I am here to judge you for being so stank sometimes. There are certain personal choices we make that become matters of public concern. One of them is not showering regularly. What is regularly? Well, for the gross and lazy, I'll say once or twice a week in the winter (when people sweat minimally) and three to four times a week in the summer. Let's use this *very* conservative timeline for the purpose of this judging and side-eye I am bestowing. Most of us need to get ourselves in somebody's tub or shower daily, but I won't be too strict right now. You're welcome.

I've heard people talk about not liking to shower, as if it were some torturous act. If you are living in a place where there is no drought and you have access to clean water, and you can't bring yourself to shower more than once a week, then I'll just assume you're allergic to water. Again, see me being considerate of you? I'm so generous.

Jesus invented soap so that we might all elect to smell like essence of lavender and vanilla whenever we want. Sure, we skip a day here and there because we're not leaving the house. But eventually we get to a point where our bodies will ring the alarm to tell us that we are officially in need of a scrubdown. That alarm bell might sound like any of the following:

1. When your armpit smell wafts by your nose from time to time

You know when you raise your hand to grab the cereal on top of the fridge and you wonder what that funk is, but then you realize that the smell is coming from your actual body? There is an odor emanating from the pocket below your shoulder, and it is of onion rings. You want to cuss yourself out so bad because all you had to do was swipe on deodorant, and you didn't even manage that. SHAME ON ME, I MEAN, YOU! Get your ass in the bathroom!

2. When you scratch your neck and your nails get dirty

You absent-mindedly scratch your chin and then look at your nails, which are now harboring an unpleasant line of dirt. Or you scratch your neck and you have to get a toothpick to dislodge whatever grossness is under your fingernails. GAHTDAMB, is that my skin? Yes it is, you middle-class, no-excuse-having hobo. That is the embodiment of your current state of filth, and you have got to get your shit together. This state of affairs means your dead skin is ready to fall off your body because you haven't washed. It is hanging on for dear life. Yes. You are harboring skin that is deceased and ready to be buried. Ew.

3. When you go to the bathroom and you catch a whiff of something unpleasant

Sometimes, we've all found ourselves in this predicament: times of heartbreak, deep depression, or being a writer. SHIT HAPPENS. But then we drag ourselves into the bathroom, ashamed that we've let ourselves rot from the outside, and we handle the situation. We wash like we were made to do so; we wash like we're going to be graded on it. We wash like Idris Elba called and said he's coming over and he's hungry but you don't need to cook (*Heeeyyy now!*). We emerge, having exfoliated layers of dirt, grime, and skin that we were meant to have shed three showers ago, feeling refreshed and unashamed. And hoping that the person who walked into our bathroom and asked if a rat died will never have reason to ask that question again. You shouldn't want your humble abode to reek of jock strap and jock itch.

There are still people who go to the bathroom without washing their hands. Some of these people work in restaurants we frequent, because why else would those "Employees Must Wash Hands" signs exist everywhere? It means people need reminders to wash their hands before handling other people's food and after they've handled nature's calling. I MEAN, COME ON! You literally just wiped your nethers. Your hands came in close proximity to the places where urine and poo come out. And you just exit the bathroom like nothing happened, like your levels of hand bacteria didn't just skyrocket? No! Not like this, beloved. Take the twenty (again, a low standard) seconds to cleanse your hands before leaving.

When my day is over and I'm about to change into my pajamas, I always wash my hands. I give it that rub-your-palms-together-for-one-minute-straight-and-squeeze routine, and I am always grossed out by how brown the water is. It doesn't matter how many times I've washed my hands that day (every time I go to the bathroom), I always have to ask myself if I freelance as a mechanic and spent five hours working under someone's hood. WHY IS IT SO DIRTY? Because we are walking dust bunnies.

This is also why women who refuse to wash their bras regularly need to be sat down and read their bill of personal rights. There are women who admit to only washing their bras once a year. WHO ARE YOU MONSTERS? RAISE YOUR HANDS SO I CAN SHAME YOU. I'm not talking about that fancy lace bra that you break out on your monthly date night. You know the one that you can only wear with black underwear because no store sells boyshorts that exact shade of aubergine? I'm not talking about that one. It only stays on for an hour and a half before the lace starts cutting into your sides and it gets removed (preferably by someone else). Your special lace bra is still looking, smelling, and feeling brand-new, so I can see why you wouldn't wash it often, I guess.

I'm talking about your favorite bra that looks fantastic under all your shirts, and you find yourself in at least once a week (sometimes twice). *That* bra you should be washing regularly. Why do I have to say this? You might be wondering, too. The answer is because of the aforementioned grown women who admit to only washing their bras once a year. I tell no lies. This is why I have to say this. This is why I judge. *Just because you can't see the dirt doesn't mean it's not there.* We can't see gravity, but here it is, holding us down like the ride-or-die partner of life. In what world does it make sense to go 365 days before washing any undergarment that has been worn? How is that even okay? An entire year of invisible debris and skin flakes just sitting on and around and beneath your underwire as you walk the streets? I know etiquette classes are so passé and all, but do we need to start hygiene schools? Where have we gone wrong? What can we do to fix it?

There should be a horror movie called *Attack of the Skin Flakes* about someone who goes an entire year without washing her bra. If we want to go the redemption route, it can be a romcom called *Loving Me and My Skin Scales.* Or a reality TV show called *For the Love of My Dead Epidermis.*

Odds are you've sweated at some point over the course of a year, so the bra has accumulated all types of musk. You might think because you've let it dry and Febreezed it all is well. That isn't how this works, ma'am. That isn't how any of this works. Why are you not washing your boob fedoras regularly? That's gross. A bra you only wash once a year must smell like bad cheese and bad decisions, like New York in the middle of summer.

I'm sure you think it doesn't smell at all. Because you know what's unreliable? Our sense of smell when it comes to our own selves. Step into someone else's house and you'll be able to smell what they last cooked, or at least describe what it smells like. But ask most people to describe the way their own house smells and they'll probably say "normal." Why? Because we get used to our own funk. Ask science. So folks who think their bras are perfectly fine might be emitting all types of odors they aren't aware of.

And can we talk about ashiness? I was minding everyone's business when I saw this dude in shorts, and his legs were downright chalky from lack of lotion. He was white, so I'm not sure if he thought that excluded him from the need to moisturize. He probably thought ashiness would blend in, but his skin was being real petty by being all "You're white, but I can get whiter in certain parts." I immediately grabbed the Vaseline in my bag and reapplied some on my own legs in case it was contagious. I needed the armor of petroleum jelly because who Jah bless with cocoa butter, no man curse with ashiness. Amen, saints.

My childhood is full of memories of my mom slathering me down from head to toe before school so I was a walking, talking oil slick. I should have realized this at the time so I could have escaped more. If she tried to catch me, I would have just slid out her grasp. Damb. I could have had adventures.

Although, no matter what you do, you find that space between your thumb and pointer finger chalky always. It's there to test your determination to remain moisturized. Don't let it win. Wash your hands, and while it's wet, slather some baby oil on it. You're welcome.

In this day and age, there is no excuse for walking around looking like you rolled in flour. With all the technology at your fingertips, you can't Google somewhere that sells aloe vera or shea butter? No excuse. You should not look as though when you exhale, a puff of dust will come out. Some people walk around looking so ashy that I assume their very soul is parched. GET THEE SOME LOTION! I just want to push them into a tub of Crisco and jojoba oil. Think about your aging process. Lifelong full-body salving is why Black folks look so young. Black doesn't snap, crackle, or pop— why? Because: moisture. It's why some of us look twelve at thirty. Listen to me, white folks. I'm dropping life secrets here. Why else do you think the Olsen twins (born in 1986) look the same age as Nia Long (born in 1970)? You haven't used the BUTTERS.

If I look at you and think I got cataracts because you look like you're in a fog from lack of emollience, I will be upset. I think my glasses are smudged, when the real reason they're looking dusty is because they didn't use some salve. You can do better than this.

Have you ever seen lips so chapped that when the person smiles too wide they start to bleed? That's me every January in Chicago if I don't apply ChapStick every thirty minutes without fail. If I go forty-five minutes, my lip situation gets compromised and I end up looking like I got into a fight and lost. And it's kinda awkward to explain to people that the fight I got into was with the weather.

Good times.

But wait. I need to go back, because clearly I'm touched by this. If people are going a whole year without washing their bras, how often do they wash their jeans? There are probably people who have *never* washed their denim pants. There's probably so much denim in the world that can stand up on its own, anchored by the dirt of a thousand wearings. Gahtdambit, everybody. Can you launder those at least once in five years? Is that too much to ask?

Don't walk around looking like Pigpen and leaving a cloud of funk in your wake. That's not okay. Get your grimy self into the bathroom and purify yourself in the waters of non–Lake Minnetonka. Wash the things you wear. Use lotion so you don't age like Benjamin Button when he was five (but looked eighty-five). Do not create denim mutant robots because you act allergic to laundry detergent. That's all. I'm not asking for too much.

Better: we must does it.

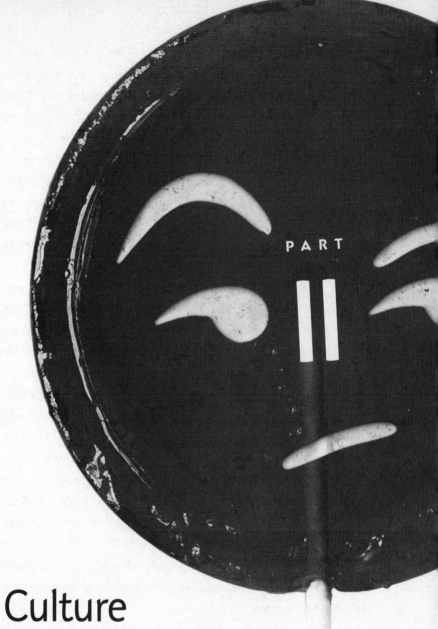

PART

II

Culture

I am a Nigerian-born, American-raised Black woman who is straight. I'm Christian, I'm walking without any assistance, and I've never been poor. This is how I identify myself, and these are the spaces I take up. Every piece of my identity is important to me and has absolutely played a role in who and where I am today. My life has been made easier by many of these things, and made harder by several others. Of course, my own hard work has gotten me here, too, but I have not had as many obstacles thrown in my way in the race of life as others have.

There are seven billion of us on this earth, and we are all different. But one thing is clear: humans excel at using our differences as excuses to act like assholes and torment one another. It is highly unfortunate that we use these innate, integral, and often uncontrollable things to mistreat others. We have created rigid, yet often invisible, systems that keep some people at the top, on the backs of others at the bottom, based on their identity markers. And we refuse to fix these systems of inequality because being at the top of the food chain is the place to be, so who would want to lose those perks? The air up there is so nice, who cares about those in the gutter?

I am judging all of us for being shitty humans by being culture vultures, homophobic jackasses, racist trolls, sexist douchebags, and born-again hypocrites.

Racism Is for Assholes

When your empire grows out of soil fertilized with the blood of a people, it must sustain its power with their continued bloodshed. The United States of America was built on the backs of Black and brown people, and it still stands on our necks. This is why I'm judging this country for the racism that permeates everything about it. It's why those of us who are melanin-rich often cannot have nice things, like freedom, equality, and liberty. CAN WE LIVE?

As I write this, a Black church is burning in South Carolina, and crews are fighting to put the fire out. This church is the seventh in two weeks that has been set aflame, and I am in a state of disbelief that in my lifetime, I am seeing this happen. This is what I read about in textbooks when I was in high school, and I'd shake my head and thank those freedom fighters who came before me for standing tall and facing those flames so I would not have to live in that type of world. I read the story of the four little girls who went to Bible study in Birmingham, Alabama, only to be blown to their deaths when their church was firebombed. I could not fathom how it would feel to live in a world where deadly hatred would meet people even in their sanctuaries. That is, until June 17, 2015, when nine people who were at church, praising God, were shot and killed by a white man, a racist terrorist.

In Charleston, South Carolina, a small Bible-study group was praying to the Lord on an otherwise uneventful Wednesday at Emanuel AME Church, the oldest Black church in the South. A white supremacist walked in, pretending to want to pray with them, and then pulled out a gun and murdered nine Black worshippers in cold blood. It was an invasion of a place of refuge, a violation of a literal safe space, and definitive proof that there is still a war on Black people in America. Nowhere is safe for us. The work that has been done over half a century to get us closer to equality has regressed, and it feels like we're back to where we started. And now another one of our churches is burning. *In 2015.*

America is treating Black people like vermin, and it's hard not to feel like we're unwanted and unsafe. It is open season on Black people, and that was not some lone gunman who walked into Emanuel AME. He represents the ongoing commitment to keep us in our place—a violent reminder that we are not safe. We are not safe in the streets, in our homes, at the park, or at church. And I am fucked up about it because this was supposed to be history—not the present—and I feel the anger from the top of my head as it reverberates down to my toes. This rage makes my skin burn. I feel the fire in my bones.

This is racism at its worst. It is ugly, demented, and vile. It also permeates every fiber of what the United States is made of, and it is what built the foundation of this country. It is like a cockroach you think you've killed, but every time you go to your bathroom at night, you see it chilling all brazen on the sink. And you're like, *Didn't I spray you with Raid and stomp on you in my steel-toed boots? What are you doing here?!* Police have body-slammed young

Black girls who were swimming at pools and killed countless unarmed people for the crime of living while Black. There have been nooses spotted hanging around college campuses, and there are 892 hate organizations currently active in the United States, the majority of which promote white supremacy. There was a viral video of a fraternity of white boys singing songs about not letting "niggers" in. Now we have to deal with the bitter cherry on the tragic sundae of oppression with the denigration of our churches and the murder of worshippers. Who in the hell left these hateful gates open?

It is truly exhausting, and I'm not sure if I'm thankful for the undeniable proof that racism is still all around us, or wishful for the days when we could be tricked into thinking things were not so bad. But racism is not just random individuals burning churches and Black people being gunned down in the streets by cops. It is a system of oppression that is so deep and omnipresent that it seeps into every single aspect of our lives, and it is as American as apple pie drizzled with canned cheese, topped with french fries. The red stripes on the flag are really the blood of Black and brown people, and many centuries after the country's creation, these stains still have not faded. The history of this country is like *Grimm's Fully Fucked-up Tales of Prejudice.*

And let's pause here to say that racism in America is stupid as hell. Racism and prejudice anywhere is dumber than wearing a wool bathing suit in the ocean. It always makes no fucking sense, but it's especially absurd here. The United States of America is a country founded on the labor and literal bodies of Black and brown people who were minding their own business when white folks came forth to kill and exploit them. This is a place that was "discovered" by a dude who didn't know how to read a map, so he just showed up on some shore, thought he was in India, and then proceeded to plant a flag there, like, "TA-DA." No, sir, no. What Christopher Columbus's goofass needed was a compass and a clue for being so aggressively mediocre, but that dude has a federal holiday in his honor. He showed up on someone else's property and claimed it as his *because he didn't know what it was*. This country started off all the way wrong and continued in the same fashion.

Chris an' 'em then slaughtered Native Americans, wiping out whole tribes, pillaging a people, and called it Thanksgiving. So much awful, so little time. Then, to add to the mess, the dudebros realized they didn't even have the ability to build dope shit on their own. So they went to Africa and captured Black people and brought them here to be their slaves—after killing millions on the journey here, of course. Because if you wanna out-terrible yourself, you stuff millions of human beings inside ships, refuse to feed them, let them lie in their own filth, and let them die in droves. So not only did you steal someone else's home and then kill them when they showed you kindness, you went elsewhere and did some more stealing, this time of actual people, and forced them to come to your STOLEN HOUSE to do your work for you. What the fuck, white people? I mean really, what in the ever-loving fuck? By the way, you're welcome for this "too long; didn't read" version of imperialism in America. This is why I should teach. Honestly, I wouldn't do any worse than current textbooks. Like the ones in Texas that used the word "workers" instead of "slaves" in the section about the transatlantic *slave* trade. As if Black people were at a career fair in Africa where we submitted résumés and asked to be beaten and starved and have our families broken in exchange for a journey across the ocean and NO MONEY. At least I'd try to be a little bit accurate.

My point is that the United States does not have a legitimate history of integrity and fairness. It's been run by villains that make Disney's look like saints. Racism is not a byproduct as much as it's the foundational stock in the American soup. This is why Black people are still fighting to be recognized in our full humanity. The success of the country has been based on our oppression, so of course it is forever fresh out of dambs to give about Black lives. We are left to grieve for those we've lost to the grubby hands of white supremacy, we rage about the perpetual cycle of mourning we find ourselves in, and we wonder what we need to do to be secure in our own skins.

How do we fight racism and racial injustice? I am not sure, but I think part of it has to be that racists recognize themselves and that everyone sees how they are contributing to the system. Let's just throw all the cards on the table.

First of all, even nice people can be racists, because racism does not depend on malicious intent. It is not a requirement for you to consciously hate someone who is of a different skin color for you to be racist. Let me repeat. You do not need to actively hate someone who is of a different race than you to do racist crap and hold racist views. Prejudice can be subconscious, like a reflex to clutch your purse tighter when that Black boy walked into the elevator you were on. Racism doesn't just look like people in white hoods who are on lawns burning crosses and churches, yelling out "nigger," and rocking blackface on Halloween for laughs. In fact, the idea that this cartoonish bigotry is what racism looks like is why some people think it is all gone and we have nothing to worry about.

The real scaffolding of racism is institutions that are so fully entwined with prejudice that to change them would require overhauling entire systems, entire ways of life. When keeping Black and brown people marginalized literally elevates white people, as they use our backs as stairs, why would they want us to stand up? *White* supremacy is ultimately the point of racism, so it is not something that *Black* people can will or wish away. We cannot respectably dress it away, un-cuss it away, protest it away. *White* people have to do it. They have to be willing to come off their (stolen) high horses and fight for change. This is why we need allies who will get uncomfortable. We need people who can look at their friends and family members and stop them in the middle of their racist jokes. It will not be comfortable to speak up, but if allies do not confront those closest to them, how do we progress?

Racism is not always white hoods and burning crosses. Sometimes, it's suits and boardrooms.

We Black and brown people are told to work twice as hard to get half as far, because we never stop auditioning for the jobs we have and we can never stop proving that we belong in the rooms we work our way into. Otherwise, we're suspected of being beneficiaries of quota systems and affirmative action. Racism is our names on our résumés being perceived as less competent and resulting in half as many job-interview callbacks as others with identical qualifications. It is the fact that Black people with college degrees often make the same as or less than a white person with a high school diploma. For women, we talk about glass ceilings; for Black people, there's often an iron gate. For Black women, well, we've got a glass ceiling with iron reinforcements.

Racism is not always white hoods and burning crosses. Sometimes, it's blue uniforms and black robes.

There's way too much haste to imprison Black women, men, and children. So much so that police will cuff (and sometimes kill) Black children that they incorrectly perceive to be a threat. The all-too-common perception that Black kids are just short adults, prone to criminal activity, is especially heartbreaking. They are treated and often tried as adults. Racism is in the case of two ten-year-olds playing in the street near their homes and ending up in handcuffs because two police officers accused them of trespassing—in their own neighborhood. How many little white boys experience that? It is the death of *Tamir Rice*, a twelve-year-old boy playing on swings at the playground while holding a BB gun. The cop who drove up to him got out of his car and shot him dead in seconds. The cop thought the gun was real and found no reason to try to resolve this situation nonviolently. Tamir was a Black boy, so that cop figured he had superpowers to kill him despite his being a child. There are countless examples of white adults pointing REAL guns at police and living to stand trial. Or even better, being talked down and taken to psych wards. But Black children are seen as dangerous criminals that people need to be protected from.

I'm kinda impressed that they think we're all superheroes who can fashion weapons out of pieces of gum, dice, and bags of chips. I am almost flattered that they think that our DNA has been X-Men-mutated so we are able to squad up at any moment. But no. Unfortunately, it's this idea that Black people are inherently violent and destructive that has been killing us for a long time. Mistaken ideas, entrenched in racism, are literally killing Black people.

It is why we have to have conversations with our kids early about how to move in America as a Black person. When we make a wrong move, like not obeying a command quick enough, or even obeying too quickly, it is a matter of life and death. It's like we're playing survival of the meekest, because as a Black person in America, you might die one day from *seeming* like a threat to someone, when you're just standing on a corner. Your very presence is frightening for no damb reason. And that fear can justify violence against you. The fact is, it is not safe to be a Black person in America.

What wounds my spirit the most is that these cops walk away without punishment, getting free vacations and high fives for killing Black people. They get *rewarded* for executing unarmed Black people. These authority figures use their power to uphold the system of brutality. We are forced to know our place, because if we don't, our safety, freedom, and lives are at stake. When Black people assert our agency by challenging or questioning police, even when we are within our rights to do so, we could lose things and people we love. How do we navigate a world that wants us to do nothing else but submit to its will?

A woman was stopped for not signaling properly while changing lanes in her car. She questioned why the cop was detaining her after he gave her a ticket, and he made her get out of the car, mishandled her, and arrested her. She spent three days in jail but never made it out—the police say she committed suicide. Whether or not she killed herself in the cell, she was murdered by an unjust system. ***Sandra Bland.*** Some people said she brought it on herself for arguing, when what she did was assert her legal rights.

Two people can commit identical crimes, and if one is Black, their punishment will likely be harsher. We make up 12 percent of the U.S. population, yet we're fully half of those in prison. We're used as convenient scapegoats for crimes, even when we're not involved. We are all disposable, and when something bad happens, blaming the Negro Boogeyman is always a safe bet. He's always described the same way, too: medium build, brown skin, short haircut. He sounds kinda hot and I wonder if he's single.

Meanwhile, white people can cuss out cops, wave guns in their faces, even assault them, and walk away with probation at the end of it. The complexion for protection is real, and when coupled with affluenza, what you have is a racist-as-hell criminal justice system. When you're white, breaking the law might get you escorted home by a cop who wants to make sure you get there safe. When you're Black, you might end up dead and gone.

Racism is not always white hoods and burning crosses. It is behind teachers' desks and in principals' offices.

Black students are three times more likely to be suspended and expelled from school than white ones. There are three-year-olds being kicked out of school for essentially being rambunctious babies. Separate has never meant equal, and public schools in majority-minority neighborhoods are being defunded. Kids are using outdated textbooks and sitting in overcrowded classrooms with overworked teachers. Yet they are being held to the same educational standards as those who have much more.

Racism is not always white hoods and burning crosses.
It is on anchor desks and in headlines.

The media has been the spokesperson for oppression since forever. It is the mouthpiece of prejudice, and it has easy access to us all, telling the stories, framing the narratives, and highlighting only what serves the larger prerogative. Racism is in easy-to-miss things like when a large group of white people gather, they are referred to as "revelers," but a bunch of people of color are called "rioters." It is what's at work when people of color are called "immigrants" and white people are referred to as "expatriates." Words mean things, and the ones they use for us are usually negative.

Racism is visible in the reporting of crimes committed by Black people way more frequently than those committed by white folks, creating the widely accepted perception that we are the face of delinquency. In spite of the fact that mass shootings are largely committed by white men, the language used for those crimes is often neutral and doesn't pathologize the criminal's fellow whites for crimes committed by an individual. White criminals are treated much more fairly, their crimes even justified by sympathetic media. If you're white, you can shoot up an entire movie theater, walk out with your life intact, and get painted as someone who is "disturbed" and worthy of pity. You kill nine Black people in a church and admit that you did it because you wanted to start a race war, and the press might report that they still cannot figure out what your motives were. You can shoot up a Planned Parenthood and be described later on as a "gentle loner."

Racism is in the media calling every brown person who commits a crime in which two or more people died a "terrorist" before the facts of the case are known, yet when a white man flies a commercial plane full of passengers into a mountain, the word "terrorist" rarely appears in any coverage about him.

Because the media has done its job so well, folks will parrot these fear-mongering and ignorant justifications for the mistreatment of Black and brown people. People feel the need to point out that crime rates are often higher in black communities, so I guess we should be used to it or something? Let's talk for a minute about how "Black on Black crime" is not a valid argument for anything. Ninety-four percent of murders of Black people are committed by other Black people, and 86 percent of murders of white people are committed by other white people. Why? Because we mostly interact within our racial groups. People victimize other people who look like them. You might as well talk about white-on-white crime, too, but you've been led to believe that Black people are somehow special in this terrible way. We are not. Also, any Black crime is *handled* by the system. In fact, it's *overhandled*. Our prisons are full of Black men and women who are in there for things as small as stealing candy bars. The system doesn't like Black folks getting away with *anything*. So you ain't gotta worry about that.

The media's obsession with "Black-on-Black crime" is just one of the many ways to blame Black victims of violence for their own victimization. They ask what the victim may have done to deserve being shot in the back, killed while in bed, choked until he could not breathe. They ask whether the cop was acting in self-defense. They actively participate in smearing the deceased, posting pics of him trying to look tough, frowning at the camera. As if every teenager doesn't have a picture of themselves mean-mugging.

When people of color are killed or we become victims of gross injustice, people ask what we did to bring it on ourselves. We seem to always ask for it, as if people go out looking for trouble that will leave them full of bullet holes, with a heart with no beat. Because to be considered a *true* victim, you need to be a saint who never even raised your voice, talked back, or took any selfies where you weren't in a choir robe. To defame your character is to place the onus for your death squarely on your shoulders. If you're in a hoodie in any of your online pics, beware. That day when you felt like rocking some Timbs and a baggy shirt? The media will find that pic and try to paint you as the "thug" they want to believe you are.

They find out that Mike/Trayvon/Tamir's stepdaddy's first cousin twice removed didn't file taxes in 2004, therefore they were dangerous monsters from a long line of criminals. There's no real correlation to the matter at hand, but that isn't important, because victims cannot be *victims* unless they were angels on earth. And when the media can't find anything vaguely negative to pin on them, they will find something on the people around them to drag their names through the mud.

Black people actually have to PROVE their humanity, instead of having it accepted as a given. Even in death, they won't let your soul rest without smearing it with dirt. But you cannot be a more "perfect" victim than to be a person in church on a weekday studying the Bible. The Charleston Nine were as saintly as we're ever likely to see. What did we do to deserve to be killed, Black people? Did we not say "please" and "thank you" enough times? Did we mouth off to a cop who then shot us in the back as we walked away? **Mike Brown**. Did we defend ourselves as we were being attacked by a random vigilante? **Trayvon Martin**. Shit, were we sleeping peacefully as police opened fire in our house looking for someone else? **Aiyana Stanley Jones**.

Then you want to add insult to injury by telling us to be calm in the face of this violence and degradation. Black trauma is never given space to heal because we have to make sure the white people who hurt us don't feel too bad about it. Even as victims, we're told to care about the feelings of those who harm us.

> Racism is not always white hoods and burning crosses. It is on Wall Street and on Capitol Hill.

It's in public policies and financial systems that keep us from getting ahead. You shoot the gun at the start of the race of life, but some of us can't even take our first step because we're chained to a pole. Then you ask why we haven't caught up to the person in front of us. Racism is when government policies defund public schools, or make accessing healthcare harder for women who are poor, or disenfranchise people who've served time in jail.

Even if today every law was reevaluated fairly, so Black people had the same rights as white folks and the barriers to access in healthcare, education, politics, and business were removed, we still would not have full equality. It's like removing you from the chains that cuffed you to that pole at the beginning of the race and telling you to catch up with everyone who's been running for, say, a few centuries already. We're not all Usain Bolt, you know. We need equity, which means taking that lack of a head start into account. Can you just give us a pair of rocket shoes so we can catch up? Thanks.

Racism is the lasting psychological, financial, and cultural legacy of centuries of slavery and segregation brought on Black people, and the lack of atonement of white people in power, and the ginormous nerve of them telling us to get over it. Maybe we'd get over it if slavery wasn't simply replaced by Jim Crow laws. Maybe we'd get over it if those laws weren't only technically removed from the books and still very much hiding in paternalistic "liberalism" and sneaky police forces. Maybe we'd get over it if Black people stop being told that things aren't that bad. *That* is how you add insult to injury. It's like when you're riding in a car with your annoying little sibling and they pinch you. You say "OUCH! Cut it out." So then they put their finger one inch from your face and say, "I'm not touching you." They might as well be, knowing damb well they're invading your personal space. Then, when you snitch on them to your parents, they say, "But I'm not touching her." YES, YOU ARE, AMERICA. YOU ARE TOUCHING ME. You might not be hanging us from trees, leaving our bodies swinging like strange fruit (hat tip to Billie Holiday), but you're killing us as we're walking down the street or sleeping in our homes or praying in church. YOU ARE TOUCHING ME, YOU OBNOXIOUS TWERP!

When Black people bring up slavery and we are told to "get over it," I want to kick every trash can in a ten-mile radius. How can we get over something that still hangs over our heads? No, we can't "get over slavery." Are Jewish people over the Holocaust? They have a right to never be, and that took fewer lives than the enslavement of Black people in America. We certainly have the right to still be mad about how much damage slavery and its continued legacy has done. You broke up families. You branded us like cattle. You killed us when we dared to want freedom. You considered us worth three-fifths of a person. You didn't want us to know how to read because you realized it'd arm us with knowledge. I just got mad about slavery all over again, and you better not say a thing to me about it. It is my right. Shoot, I specialize in holding grudges.

And then some folks have the nerve to tell us to "go back to Africa." Shut the hell up. Your ancestors brought my skinfolk over here and got us to build you some dopeness, and now you want us to go back? There's no refunds or takebacks here. Your receipt has expired and you can't even get store credit. You can't walk into Starbucks, buy a cup of coffee, drink it all, and then say you want your money back. This is as much our house as it is yours, and like Effie White, I'm not going. You don't have to love us, but you at least have to tolerate us and treat us like human beings. Otherwise, when we raise hell, don't act like you don't know why. Throwing rocks and then hiding your hands—that's some bullshit.

Those white stars are cracked and the stripes bleed. Until America is ready to turn the mirror on itself and address the giant, pink, racist elephant in the room, we cannot fix any of this.

I'm judging you, 'Murica.

The Privilege Principle

There comes a time in every upwardly mobile Black person's life when they encounter someone who tells them how "well-spoken" and "articulate" they are. It is usually a white person who is earnest and honest in their admiration of your verbal abilities, and in that moment, you swing between being appreciative and being totally offended. It's a backhanded compliment at best, but mostly it's a put-down, because no matter how much you've studied, how nice your clothes are, or how impressive your body of work is, people will still expect little from you (because: minority). It's microaggressions and instances of casual racism like this that pepper our daily lives, leaving a terrible taste in our collective mouths, and it usually comes from white folks who consider themselves to be liberal, learned, and progressive. Sometimes, I wonder which is better: a blatant bigot or an oblivious racist? At least there are no guessing games or riddles to solve with the former.

If you want to correct their "articulate" comments, you will often be met with, "Oh, I didn't mean it like that!" Ma'am. Sir. How did you mean it? Have you ever given a white colleague a pat on the back for knowing how to speak in complete sentences? No? Okay. Sometimes, the person will go on the defensive. This might be where they bring up that one Black friend they have, using them as proof that "I'm not racist." I assure you that the possibility of you socializing with Black people does nothing to take the sting away. It's the first cousin of the statement "Not to be racist, but . . ." If you ever find yourself uttering those words, go find some duct tape and put it over your mouth until the urge to complete the sentence passes. What you were about to say is not okay, so you might as well swallow it. In fact, you just won at Prejudice Bingo. You hit all the squares in the time it took to formulate that thought. Congratulate yourself by having a seat for a little while.

Racism in all its many flavors is easier to recognize and call out when it's KKK-style Original Recipe. But when the form it takes isn't slurs and hate speech thrown in your face, people don't always see it, want to acknowledge it, or understand how much it affects the everyday lives of others. After all, the road to hell is paved with good intentions, and some white people believe that because their motives aren't malicious, they surely cannot be racist or harbor prejudices. I am here to let them know that I am judging them for thinking being "a little bit" of a bigot is a thing. That's like being "a little bit diabetic."

We are all living in systems bigger than ourselves, but we have to be willing to acknowledge their existence. As engrained as racism and ethnic prejudice are in the United States (and many countries around the world), minorities still have to spend our time convincing white people that there is even a problem that needs to be fixed. Some people think that because they aren't overtly racist assholes (which, You're So Articulate Chad, is debatable) means that the larger society we live in isn't racist either, and therefore they do not recognize the privilege that allows them to even operate from that skewed belief. Being quiet about race or not wanting to acknowledge it is being a part of the problem, no matter how nonracist you personally are.

Some well-meaning folks think if we stop talking about racism, it'll magically disappear, like the smell of an errant fart. But like a fart, people might try to be polite and ignore it but everyone knows it's there. Avoidance has never been a great tactic in solving any problem. For most situations in life, not addressing what's going wrong only makes matters worse. It's like someone breaks your arm, and the person who slammed the baseball bat into it is saying, "The only reason it won't heal is because you keep complaining that it hurts." How about you get me a cast so the bone can set straight again? America does not want to put the effort into providing this cast. This is why we must talk about race, and we must do it openly.

As we rage about the system that privileges white people over people of color, that has been allowed, encouraged, and state sanctioned, we get pushback saying that not all white people are racist. Listen. We didn't say ALL white people are racist, but racism is real, bigots are plenty, and we're not just making this up to make white folks feel bad. We're saying that white people benefit from an automatic position of privilege because of their skin color in a larger racist society. We didn't call you, Individual White Person, racist, unless you feel like us pointing out the FACT of white privilege makes you a bigot. In that case, by all means, holler like hit dogs do. Racism is not just perpetuated by the people in white hoods. It's also the well-meaning "I have Black friends" people who help it remain upright and unmovable. They refuse to see the part they play in the system because they're too busy making sure everyone knows how NOT racist they are.

Listening to Black music and loving Beyoncé does not give you a free hall pass out of the system of structural racism. Just because I enjoy a salad from time to time doesn't mean I'm a vegetarian. Being able to live without having to be defined by your skin color is the hallmark of privilege. So let's talk about privilege. This word feels accusatory to many, and they feel assaulted (or insulted) by the idea of possessing it. In reality, it's not about *you*; it's about your actual factual societally supported white privilege.

Some of my favorite memories from college are from my two and a half years as a counseling center paraprofessional. We were trained peer counselors, and part of our training curriculum was to spend our first semester as CCPs learning about ourselves, our place in the world, and how it relates to others around us. This is when I was introduced to the privilege exercise, which really changed the way I view the space I take up in this world.

Our group of twenty was incredibly diverse (in color, religious beliefs, class, sexual orientation, gender identity, etc.). To begin the exercise, we all stood in a straight horizontal line across the room. When our facilitator made a certain statement, folks either took a step back, took a step forward, or stayed in place. Example: "Take a step forward if you've never had to worry about where your next meal would come from." "Take a step back if you've ever felt judged because of the color of your skin." "Take a step back if your name has ever been pronounced incorrectly." "Take a step forward if you can legally get married to the person you love." At the end of the exercise, after about thirty statements, we were told to pause, look around, and see where we were. By then, everyone was standing in different places, and we had to observe whether there was a pattern in who was in front of or behind us. You learn a lot about the people in that room with you, and you might even find someone you'd never expect standing behind you!

Unsurprisingly, the people in the very front were the straight white men in the class. I was in the middle, because I'm heterosexual, Christian, middle-class, and cisgender. The people behind me were those who identified as members of three or four marginalized groups (gay, poor, Muslim, etc.). That exercise changed my world, because it was an important lesson on how we don't all have the same opportunities, and even though we might all technically start in the same place (on paper), we quickly find ourselves behind or ahead in the world.

Our privileges are the things not within our own control that push us forward and move us ahead from that starting line. Acknowledging them does not mean you are admitting to doing something to purposefully contribute to someone else's oppression or marginalization. Nay, friends. It means you recognize that some part of your identity puts you in a better position than others. It means something about you assists your progress in the race of life. It also means that whatever majority group you belong to has likely contributed to the oppression of another. Knowing our privilege does not make us villains, but it should make us more conscious about the parts we play in systems that are greater than us. It should make us be more thoughtful; it should humble us. We need to admit that some of us had a head start and aren't just flourishing on our strength alone.

Again, YOU might not personally be responsible for the oppression of others, but you're amongst a group that is benefitting from said oppression. On the list of privileges, whiteness is arguably the biggest one. This is not an accusation but a fact that people need to recognize and acknowledge. If you are white in the United States, you carry a giant stamp of approval that has already made your life easier compared to others'. White people are in positions of power in every societal structure, and get to see themselves reflected everywhere. White privilege is not having to worry about speaking for your entire ethnicity because your behavior is perceived as yours alone, not representative of everyone who looks like you. It's characters in cartoons and video games that look like your kid, or at least only a few shades away from them. Tights and undergarments that are labeled as "nude" consider your skin the default, so it matches you, and you only, white people. Privilege is never even having to notice when you are reflected in movies or in boardrooms, because you are always reflected.

The most glaring aspect of white privilege is that when someone is described neutrally—without indicating color or ethnicity—more often than not, people will assume that the person is white. THAT assumption indicates an uncomfortable truth: in our society, whiteness determines humanity.

Unfortunately, people are so ill equipped to deal with race that some are not only unwilling to see their privilege, they're unwilling to even admit that we're all different colors. They're so committed to avoidance that these people say they don't even see color at all. I call shenanigans. Colorblindness isn't a thing. Well, medically it is. Some people have trouble distinguishing between certain colors. Even scientifically, though, colorblindness does not mean you cannot tell black from white. Random fact for you, if you ever end up on *Jeopardy* and your Daily Double depends on it: the reason Facebook's logo is blue is because Mark Zuckerberg is red-green colorblind, and shades of blue are the richest ones he can see. THE MORE YOU KNOW *shooting star*. But I bet even Zuck can tell the difference between my skin and his.

So for people to sit on some delusional "more evolved" throne and proclaim themselves colorblind, and therefore unable to be prejudiced or racist, is absurd at best, cowardice at medium (yes, medium), and dangerous at worst. "I don't see race or color. I just see people." You are lying like a good Persian rug handmade by a widow. That statement is an extra helping of wack sauce on disingenuous spaghetti. No one is lacking color. Are we water? Did Jesus walk on us or try to turn us into wine to keep the party going? No, he did not. The point of trying to be "colorblind" is not so we can deny what is obviously there; it's supposed to be so we don't treat people as less-than because of their color. But classifications and categories aren't bad in and of themselves. What's bad are the stereotypes and degradation that come with some of the categories we're a part of. The acknowledgement of the boxes that we fit in isn't wrong, and neither is the recognition of our differences.

Furthermore, eschewing our cultural differences doesn't make America or anyplace a salad bowl. It erases our history and the very relevant events of the past that have led to our present situations. It dishonors our ancestors and the work they've done. And it lets people off the hook for centuries of race-based denigration and injustice. So saying you don't see race is saying you have nothing to fix. "Colorblindness" and cultural erasure help perpetuate this crappy system of oppression, because forced politeness and fear of the "race card" trump actual work and progress. In the words of my beloved cousin (in my heart) Kerry Washington, "I'm not interested in living in a world where my race is not a part of who I am. I am interested in living in a world where our races, no matter what they are, don't define our trajectory in life." We are not supposed to be homogenous, but we should all be able to exist harmoniously, side by side, even with our differences. I want people to see my color and my culture written all over me, because I am proud of the skin I'm in. It is an important part of my identity. What I don't want them to do is mistreat me because of it.

The world itself is not blind to race, so individual claims to be such are nonsense. It's like saying you see a red traffic light as blue. AND? Everyone else sees it as red, so your supposed blue light makes no damb difference. You and everyone around you still operate like it's red, so what does your perception mean, anyway? Yes, I know race is a construct. So is Santa Claus, and yet we sit down on December 25th every year and exchange gifts that we say he brought us. Socially constructed things become real when they're embedded in the culture. Language and money are constructs, too, and yet they are also real things that have real impact in our lives. We need to deal with the constructs, not swim in cultural denial. We cannot avoid or deny our issues away and think we can actually move forward. You cannot be a part of a solution when you aren't even willing to admit there is a problem.

"Colorblindness" is an attempt to play the Get Out of Trying to Fix This Free card, the ultimate cheat code in the game of white privilege. Being able to move and navigate in the world unaware of how race impacts people of color must give life a rosy tint that makes it easier to deal with. However, it makes it harder for those of us who do not have that setting. It's the well-meaning, yet offensive aunty of the "All Lives Matter" crew, the folks who have to respond with that anytime we say "Black Lives Matter." We know all lives *should* matter, but ALL lives cannot matter until Black lives matter, too.

I'm not sure who I side-eye more, though: Team I Don't See Color or Team Let Me Honor You by Painting My Face Black for Halloween. One group thinks they're laudable for not acknowledging racial differences, and the other thinks being represented by face paint should make us feel appreciated. For the last time, white folks: Black face, red face, brown face, or yellow face *is not okay*. If there is anything that gets my blood pressure sky-high in two seconds flat, it is blackface-wearing white folks who think they're somehow paying homage to us even as they look more like creatures out of horror movies. WHITE PEOPLE, THIS IS NOT OKAY. I REPEAT: NOT OKAY!

It's not okay for the same reason that it's not okay that there's still a sports team called "Redskins." If you're reading this after 2016, and you're like "No, there isn't," then it's because we all finally got our lives together and stopped being jerkwads and changed that offensive name. You might be living in a better world, or at least one that isn't so bold in its awfulness. Congrats. But right now, the Washington Redskins are a franchise in the National Football League, despite Native Americans and allies speaking up repeatedly to say that the name is derogatory. What I don't understand is how a group of people can say, "Hey, you're offending us. Stop that!" and people can go "But it's our team name!" or "We're just having fun! Relax!" That's like if you're stepping on my toes, and I say, "Ouch—get off!" and you say, "But I've been standing on your feet for like forty minutes. I like it. I'll stay." How dare you?!

My alma mater is the University of Illinois, and up until my junior year in undergrad, Chief Illiniwek was our mascot. He was always portrayed by a white student wearing a feathered headdress who'd hop around during halftime of sports games yelling, "OSKEE WOW WOW!" When they got rid of him, people were in tears, saying, "He's a tradition!" Grown-ass people were on TV crying because our mascot, the made-up Indian chief, was being retired. Alums threatened to stop donating to the university because the RACIST. MASCOT. WAS. BEING. RETIRED! I was floored.

These people are seriously sitting around like, "Why do I need to stop painting myself black, red, brown, and yellow for laughs? Why do we need to change the racial slur that represents our sports franchise?" Here's why: because it's what good people do. They care about our feelings of hurt and pain, attached to centuries of denigration, genocide, slavery, smallpox, and every terrible thing that happened on this continent ever.

It all comes down to white people going out of their way to keep up traditions (*their* traditions) because that is what they're comfortable with. Let's remember that slavery and bondage of people of color, with beatings, rape, and slaughter, was a centuries-long tradition as well. Some things just need to be done away with.

While we are here, I want to remind non-Black people that NO, you cannot say "nigga." I know you didn't use the "-er." I know it's part of that song you really like, or your best friend is Black, or you adopted a son from Malawi. STAHP. Just stop it, right this moment. Yes, Black people might say it to each other, but *you* cannot. Words used within a marginalized group are not always appropriate when used by an outsider. We should know this already. Some members of the LGBTQ community use the F-word that rhymes with "bag" as a term of endearment. If my heterosexual ass used that word? I should be kicked in the shins. That is not *my* word to use; I don't have the right. Why? I am a member of the privileged class that has used that word to belittle gay people, so I cannot use it, no matter how many gay people do. Same with the word "bitch" and women. If a man refers to me as such, I might wanna elbow him in the chest. People who are in marginalized groups can define how they want to use words that have been historically derogatory. They can reclaim them as they deem fit. *You* sit it out, because you don't even go to this school. So cut this whole thing out. The fact that we *still* have to have this conversation is just mind-boggling, and it makes me want to lay my burdens down under a blanket.

You might be wondering, "Luvvie, how can I stop you from judging me?"

Forge some real friendships with people who don't look like you. Stop saying you don't see color and acknowledge your privilege. Also, if you've already figured all of this out, check your friends and family who have not. This is your farm, and those are your sheep. Gather them and tell them to get their shit together. Then I will stop judging you. Maybe.

Zamunda Is Not a Country.
Neither Is Africa.

It was my first week in the United States, and I was nine years old and unsure of what I was doing at school. I thought we were just visiting this country. Nobody had told me we were leaving Nigeria to go live in America. (We didn't call it "the United States." I knew it as "America.") Apparently, this wasn't going to be like the other time, when we came for two weeks; we were here to stay. My mom dropped me off at school, and the principal showed me to my classroom and introduced me to my teacher. Mrs. Chu pulled me in the door and told the class to say hi to the newest student. Then she turned to me and told me to introduce myself.

For the first time in my life, I wanted to hide myself. It was the first time I had ever been "the new girl." I mean, in Nigeria I had it so good that the headmistress of the private school I went to was my mom's best friend. In fact, my best friend's grandmother owned the school, and I had been attending it since I was two years old. So being the new girl *anywhere* was a brand-new experience. I was further betrayed by my strong Nigerian accent, which othered me immediately from my new classmates. For someone who had never had to feel like an outsider, coming from a place where everyone looked and spoke like me, it was jarring. It also didn't help that at lunch, when everyone else pulled out sandwiches from their bags, I pulled out a bowl of white rice and stew. Later on, I needed a pen and asked someone for a "Biro." I minuswell[11] have had two heads.

Growing up in Nigeria, where I wanted for nothing, I was raised to be proud of who I am. I come from a family that is well known and very respected, and I was raised to walk into rooms with my head held high because I belonged in whatever room I wanted to be in. I did not know what it was really like to doubt myself until that day, standing in front of my fifth-grade class, when I learned what it was like to have the most visible part of my identity also be the very thing that people thought was different and wrong.

At nine years old, I felt the effects of the false perception of Africa as a single entity with a single story as I navigated the new world of middle school in a new country where no one knew *my* story. They just knew I was the new African girl with the weird name and weird accent. People projected clichés onto me, asked me stupid questions, and made me feel like I had to defend my culture: "No, we don't have lions in our backyards, and yes we wear clothes." And when people would add "mon" to their sentences directed at me ("Hey, mon!"), I would wanna throat-chop them. JAMAICA IS NOT IN AFRICA, DUMBASSES. NOT THE FUCKING SAME. At least try to get the continent right! Is Google Maps busy? Well, Google Maps did not exist then. I did not know that in America being African was thought to be joke-worthy. I did not know folks would think I'd be primitive in any way, so when I heard the "African booty scratcher" jabs, I learned for the first time the stereotypes that people thought of when they saw me.

---

[11] *minuswell*: "Might as well" is just too right.

People thinking Mama Africa is a big jungle and one giant country makes me so mad! It makes me want to cunt-punt a plush teddy bear across traffic at rush hour. I am judging us for the terribly misleading and narrow views we hold about the cradle of civilization.

Anyway, as kids are so good at doing, I adapted. I learned to mimic the way my American friends spoke, and by the time I started high school, my Naija accent was mostly gone. I no longer sounded like a proper aje butta[12] Ibadan girl. I was officially a child of Chicago.

Even more significantly, I also stopped using my first name outside my house, because people made it ugly and heavy. I am Yoruba. My name is Ifeoluwa, and I love it and I wanted to protect it fiercely. It means "God's love," and it is made up of five syllables that might look confusing at first glance, but really, slowly spoken, is no tongue twister. E-FE-OH-LOO-WAH. But when people used it, it took on a sound that was unrecognizable. Soon I was going by the nickname my aunt gave me: Lovette. By high school, I was no longer pegged as a foreigner, and I blended in very well. It was a matter of pride for me, because this West African girl was not so glaringly *African* anymore. At that point, I couldn't even mimic my Naija accent if I tried.

That cheap delight in forcefully integrating myself ended when I got to college, when I met fellow African students who were unabashedly proud and spoke in their accents unapologetically. Ghanaians, Ethiopians, Nigerians, Eritreans. They embraced their cultures, and their very existence helped to diffuse whatever lingering shame I might have felt. I ended up becoming vice president of the African Cultural Association my junior year. It was a long journey to reclaim my pride in the very part of my existence I had been shamed for.

---

[12]*aje butter* (or *butta*): Phrase used to describe upper-class (sometimes spoiled) people in Nigeria.

My classmates were only reflections of a larger world that considered being African a liability because they had no understanding of the complexities of the second biggest continent in the world. All they knew was a one-dimensional Africa, and I blame the media for a lot of this.

Some years ago, I stumbled upon an episode of *Nightline* wherein the topic was an exposé on African children who were accused of witchcraft. I sat there knowing I would not be pleased with what I was about to see, but I watched anyway because the remote control was on the other side of the room. Also, I'm a glutton for punishment. The program showed children who were crying while being held by their parents as they went through exorcisms. They showed a naked child who was getting hot wax poured on him as he writhed like a snake. While the elders on my screen were rebuking the children for their supposed witchcraft, I rebuked *Nightline*, then summoned the strength to go get the remote and change the channel.

The stories the media chooses to present shape our distorted views of Africa. Of course this show highlighted barbaric behavior, naked people, an interpreter, closed captioning because no one there could speak English, and, of course, flies buzzing around. All they needed was Sally Struthers in the background looking on disapprovingly and they would have hit Africa Story Bingo.

Of course I also forget which country this exposé took place in. All I remember was that it was in Africa, and that is by design. Why should we care what area of Africa it took place in when it's just one giant country anyway, AMIRITE?

The media is complicit in Africa's monolithic story being told, amplified, and considered gospel by the world. How can you paint such a flat, broad portrait of a place where there are more languages and cultures than I can count? How can you sing one tune when you should be having multiple concerts? It's incredibly lazy. Africa has a PR problem, and Olivia Pope needs to handle it.

I begrudge the mainstream media's obsession with seemingly

"uncivilized" Africans. Between the Discovery Channel, National Geographic, and these "investigative reporters," we only seem to be told about the Africa that is disease-ridden, poverty-stricken, and without any sense of modern-day living. The kids with the dusty hair and flies buzzing around their heads are the mascots. Let the press tell it: no one in Africa thinks bras exist. All they ever show are the women with the free tits and men with the Pinocchio wee wees. MTCHEW![13] Cameramen, and the audience, sit there observing them like they're fish in an aquarium. It's on some "Crikey! Let's watch the African in his natural habitat" crap. I do not like it one bit.

I'm not saying they ought not to show the forests in Africa and the people who wear fig leaves and nothing else. Their lives are valid and their stories should be told. However, it should not be the only aspect of the Motherland that is depicted. Methinks these portrayals are ridiculous, misleading, and counterproductive when they are used to define the continent. Have you ever seen a special about the continent that was about city life? Hell, show *one* house that isn't made of mud and I may be slightly appeased. Haysoos[14] be some different viewpoints for the media and Africa.

On the other side of the distorted story is the appropriation and cultural theft of many things African, which undermines the entire "they are barbaric" thing. If we're so ass-backwards, then surely you shouldn't feel the need to look to us for new trends. As we're being shown on television as people who don't wear clothes, high-fashion designers are using ankara and dashiki fabric for their latest collections. Our geles (head ties) from Nigeria are being imitated, and folks are making YouTube videos to teach Western-

---

[13]*mtchew*: West Indians refer to this as "steupsing"—it's the sound you make when you suck your teeth in annoyance.

[14]*Haysoos*: A shout-out to the Spanish pronunciation of "Jesus."

ers how to rock them. Louis Vuitton is selling replicas of the red/blue/white plaid bags we call "Ghana Must Go" for a thousand dollars. They retail for about a hundred naira (which is like seventy cents) at Murtala Muhammed Airport in Lagos, Nigeria. It is a weird combination of appreciation, fetishization, and contempt. We're interesting and modern when our cultural markers are being co-opted but we are barbaric when it comes to how our stories are being told.

Our cultural symbols and identifiers are appreciated only when they profit people who don't look like us. We, as African people, are *studied* but not *seen*. Our beauty is viewed through a Western lens. You either have to be dark as midnight and unmistakably African to be considered beautiful or you better not think that wide nose and angled face with prominent cheekbones makes you pretty. Many of us have gotten the "You don't look African" remark because we don't look like Alek Wek. Others have gotten it from people insinuating that not looking African is some kind of compliment, which is incredibly insulting. "You're so pretty! I would not have guessed you were African." BISH, WHAT? Thanks for not thinking I'm like those other Africans. You know, the ugly ones. People can suck sometimes.

It's fascinating how bold people are about their ignorance of Africans, Africa, and anything related to it. Usually, people try to keep their stupidity subtle but not with Africa, though. Why try? Some of the questions folks will ask are so rude that replying rudely is perfectly acceptable. I got these questions from classmates when I first got to the United States, but I've also heard some of these questions from adults, full-grown people who should know better. Some folks know more about the gahtdamb moon than the continent that is only ten hours away from them by plane. *HOW, SWAY?*

For my fellow Africans, here's a handy Q&A response guide for you to use next time someone hits you with one of these frequently asked queries:

Do you have cars where you're from? Who needs cars when you have goats? That's perfectly good transport! For extra-big people we use baby elephants.

Do you wear clothes at home? Yeah, we wear clothes in Chicago. Oh, you mean in Nigeria? Nah. The only time we wear things like pants or anything that covers our asses is when we have to ride our goats. Since it's so hot, the leather saddles heat up and can cause third-degree burns. And we only wear shirts when we have to go to church to worship the god of the moon. Sundays are honored by showing no nipples, so we put on our leaf tank tops to pray.

Yes, we wear clothes. Many of us even have seamstresses who make our clothes and also our aso ebi [Yoruba phrase that literally translates to "clothes of kin"] for special occasions like weddings, birthdays, Wednesdays, etc. This is why you see family pictures of us all wearing matching fabric in different styles. We are about this *alphet*[15] life! We also wear jeans and T-shirts and suits. SURPRISE!

Is there a lion in your backyard? Yes. In fact, that scene where Mufasa was telling Simba not to go to that shadowy area was a reenactment. He was talking about our nosy next-door neighbor's property. The one who wears leaves with unholy nipple cutouts on Sundays. She doesn't have any respect. I also heard her leaves were made in China. Traitor.

Do you speak African? When did you learn to speak English? I used to be fluent in African, then I learned American, and now I'm trying to learn Asian, so I can be trilingual. Anyway, I was determined to learn this language they referred to as "English," so I went to the one library on the continent of Africa, headed to the Restricted Books section, and pulled out the only book in English, which was *The Cat in the Hat*, and read it for many months. OR

---

[15]*alphet*: Because it's more fun to say than "outfit." Now that you know this word, you cannot unknow it. You're welcome!

maybe I learned to speak English from birth, and it is as much my first language as Yoruba is. Go have a damb seat.

How did your hut fit your whole family? Our hut was a nine-bedroom house. We managed, against all odds. We thank God. And Orisha.

Did you have electricity? This little light of mine is all I need to let shine. Besides, who needs electric light when you have the sun? When the sun comes up, we start our day. If the sun is down, we have no need for light, for we are a people of the earth.

Who is the president of Africa? President Olu Obama, of course. He's Barack's third cousin. He rules the Republic of Africa with an iron fist.

How did you get here? From Nigeria I swam to France, then hopped on a train to London. Then my mom worked as a waitress for five years, saved up money, and bought tickets on a ship coming to the United States. But then our tickets got stolen, so we had to stow away on the ship. Three years later, we made it to the Promised Land.

* * *

These questions would be fun to shoot down if their absurdity didn't illustrate how insultingly misguided people are about Africa. Folks thinking that because *Coming to America* is their favorite movie they know all they need to know about the continent. Someone somewhere believes it was a documentary about a kingdom named Zamunda. I just KNOWED it. If I facepalmed as often as I want to, I'd have a permanent indentation on my forehead. It doesn't end with young children being curious about lions or folks believing there are professional royal penis cleaners. It goes to the hearts and minds of people in positions of power who create policy and of regular folks who think they're open-minded when they are anything but.

The way the 2014–2015 Ebola epidemic was handled and reacted to by people around the world perfectly encapsulates how problematic and racist the single (scary) story about Africa is. When the Ebola epidemic started in Sierra Leone in 2014, ravaging communities, taking lives, and leaving children orphaned, the Western world paid very little attention. We had very few fucks to give, because it was an African people problem. Then the epidemic moved to Liberia, and still there was little alarm on this side of the ocean. But when Ebola finally made its way to Dallas, Texas, through a man who did not know he was infected until after he flew here, shit got real. He shattered everyone's safety bubble in an instant—a fake-ass bubble if I ever saw one.

Two American doctors who got infected while treating patients in Liberia were airlifted and taken to Emory University Hospital in Atlanta, and the panic peaked as people wondered why we were allowing the virus to be brought closer to home. Apparently, while it was contained to certain regions of West Africa it was okay, because that was far away. People wondered why the Centers for Disease Control wouldn't want to "keep that in Africa." Oh, okay—let's not use the best modern medicine has to offer to see how it can be handled better everywhere. Let's not have the brightest scientific minds try to curtail an outbreak for the good of the whole world.

Ebola wasn't "our" problem before that moment, but we forget that the entire world is now no more than a twenty-four-hour plane ride away. Air travel makes the world tiny, and something on one side of the world is less than a day away. So we were never as protected from Ebola as people thought. The Ebola hysteria got so real that people stopped traveling to all parts of Africa—even places where the virus had never been present. Canceling travel to Tanzania because Ebola is in Liberia is like saying you won't go to Canada because England is having a bird flu outbreak. A teacher in Kentucky was forced to resign because she traveled to Kenya during the panic, when the virus never even made it to freaking

Kenya! How the hell does that even make sense? People proposed barring all incoming travel from West Africa. Stigma is a bitter bitch.

Countries that were nowhere near the outbreak saw their tourism revenues plummet because of people thinking that Africa is one giant country and a sneeze in Sierra Leone can travel five thousand miles to South Africa. Foolishness abounds. The media stoked the fire, and it was all irresponsible as hell. Everyone who was on a plane and coughed was profiled as a possible carrier of the virus, and all of it was just panic. There were only five cases *total* in the United States, and the only fatality was the initial patient from Liberia. We all breathed a sigh of relief because we had dodged a bullet. We didn't even look back to see who we had left behind. We did not try to help address the infrastructure issues in rural communities in Sierra Leone, Liberia, and Guinea that spurred the epidemic on. That was not our business, right?

It's funny how folks insist on being hands-off with only *certain* issues in Africa. The world hasn't always been so shy in meddling all up in the continent's business for centuries. Hell, colonialism was just global gentrification on steroids. The Dutch, the Spaniards, the French, and the British were on some nosy-neighbor bullshit and carrying themselves to the Motherland to "save the people." They weren't so laissez-faire then. The Dutch came up on the shores of South Africa and thought it was beautiful, so they parked their asses on the land and decided to never leave. I've been to Cape Town, so I can see why you would want to stay forever, because it is magnificent, but that's bold. It's like me liking your shoes, taking them off your feet, and declaring them to be mine now. That's BOLD!

Folks have not minded their business when it most mattered, running through Africa drawing arbitrary borders and planting flags since forever. Even in 2014, a random white dude from Virginia took himself to Sudan, picked a plot of land, and named it the Kingdom of North Sudan, all because his daughter said she wanted to be a princess. I don't know why he didn't just go to Burger King and get her a paper crown. You can actually still go around the world putting janky homemade flags in places and declaring them to be yours? Did we fall into a hole in the space-time continuum and end up in the 1400s, before we had all figured out the guidelines to this "country" thing? White folks, y'all gotta quit this shit. Columbussing is so 1492. And the fact that it can still happen in Africa is absurd. History is crowded with people who just randomly showed up in Africa and grabbed some land, like the cradle of civilization is a Monopoly board. There are too many countries on the continent that celebrate fifty-year (or less) national anniversaries because they just recently got independence from Britain, Spain, or France. The only African country to have never been under colonial rule at any point is Ethiopia.

Robbing a place of its resources and pilfering the land dry can get tiring after a couple of centuries, so when colonialists decided to be done with wherever they had conquered, they left behind political, socioeconomic, and class-structure issues that rendered countries in shambles. In their wake they left deadly civil wars stemming from forcing clans and ethnic groups with major differences under the same umbrella. But when shit hits the fan and problems develop from the legacy of colonialism—like a butterfly effect, if the butterfly was really an elephant that flipped tables and ruined everything—then the colonizers want to say it's not their business. They want to play Captain Save-a-Hoe when it comes to pilfering the land of its wealth, but when it's time to offer the countries on the continent actual aid, they come up missing like we do when Sallie Mae calls asking about our student loan payments. I call bullshit.

Just like African problems are thought to belong in Africa only and to be the sole responsibility of the people there, African people outside of the continent must assimilate or face rejection. It is frustrating to see how people approach things regarding Africa and Africans in such alienating ways, even the way people look at our names and cringe before they try to pronounce them. Like my classmates when I first arrived in the United States, people's tongues get heavy with the pressure of the hardship they assume comes with multiple vowels and more than six letters, and you can see their shoulders slump in expected failure. You'd think you just asked someone to take a surprise SAT test. People see our names and automatically assume they'll be tongue-twisted.

I used to hate the first day of school, when the teacher would be taking roll and would get to "Ajayi." I would know it was me before they even said my name because I was almost always first on the list, and almost without fail, my teacher would look up and say, "This is a hard name." This is when I would say, "It's probably me," and dread having to pronounce my unique name while all the other kids watched me, eyebrows raised with curiosity. It is AJAYI. Pronounced AH-JA-YEE. There are no tricks. I used to wish I had a simple name like "Lauren Jones" because I got sick of standing out on the first day of school. Sometimes, the teacher would ask, "Is there something else I can call you?" because learning how to say my first name correctly was just too cumbersome, I guess. If they could not pronounce "Ajayi," then surely "Ifeoluwa" was their auditory nightmare, so I gave them an alternative. Feeling like you have to go by an alias so the world doesn't butcher your beautiful real name sucks.

I still remember my high school graduation and how my vice principal botched my name. He had no excuse, especially since he had the phonetic spelling written on a notecard *and* we had prac-ticed the day before. He called my name, and the only reason I knew it was mine was because I was next in line. I might have looked around momentarily for the person who he just called. I was all "Dang, her name is ugl— Oh, that's me." My last name is not even hard. It's one of the easier Nigerian ones. I always say, "It's pronounced just like it's spelled." Still, folks look at it and go, "Ay-jay." Don't ignore my I, bro! I have been on the phone with cus-tomer service reps multiple times where I've had to spend three minutes teaching them how to say my last name. *Ah-jay. Ah-ya-jee. Ah-jay-ya.* Ma'am, it is Ah-JAH-YEE. Yet folks can say Schwarzenegger or Galifianakis without a problem. It makes no sense whatsoever.

How African names are approached by many Americans and the barrier of entry to even saying them feels like more othering. We have learned to say much harder names. We have learned phonetic rules of other tongues while ignoring the fact that a lot of African names still follow English pronunciation rules. By doing this, we're telling people that their African names are too difficult and not worth learning how to say correctly. We tell them their culture is a nuisance to our Western tongues and we force people to either abandon their real monikers or be faced with people who are annoyed at having to make an effort. It's disrespectful.

When we look at a map, North America seems worlds away from Africa. But that distance is less about the miles between the two and more about the strangeness attributed to the continent's people. Honestly, we live in bubbles of ethnocentrism, and we carry around ideas and stereotypes about places we've never been. Like my shero Chimamanda Ngozi Adichie said, "The single story creates stereotypes, and the problem with stereotypes is not that they are untrue, but that they are incomplete. They make one story become the only story." That single story has painted a broad stroke of gloom and doom on Africa's canvas, and I want people to see beyond that disingenuous caricature.

I wrote this chapter while I was on vacation. My view was of the mountains in front of me and an infinity pool to my left. There was a Givenchy Spa in the hotel lobby, and the people around me mostly spoke French. There was a wind that was cooling me from the hot sun. I was eating seafood linguini as I restarted my iPad so I could connect to the hotel Wi-Fi. This was in Africa (Fez, Morocco, specifically). So was the national park where I spotted a giraffe and a hyena (Nairobi, Kenya). So was the beach that doubled as a penguin colony where I watched the little tuxedoed birds waddle around (Cape Town, South Africa). So was the site of the weeklong tech conference that was a part of a global network in a modern, bustling city (Lagos, Nigeria). So was the shantytown where the houses had tin roofs (Malabo, Equatorial Guinea).

These places are all Africa, because it is a continent with fifty-four countries, hundreds of landscapes, and thousands of languages spoken by people across countless cultures. Fourteen percent of the world's population can be found there. The entire United States, China, and India can fit comfortably in the continent with room left over. Africa is north, south, east, and west. Three oceans touch its borders. Africa is amazing. I mean, come on. Science has traced the first humans back to the continent, and civilization is thought to have begun there. The place is rich with oil, diamonds, and jollof rice. It is not a monolith, and it is not solely populated by helpless people who need to be pulled from the depths of misery. There are feasts and famines. There are prosperity and poverty. There are democracies and dictatorships. The continent is much greater than the sum of its single parts.

Africa is home to such beauty and cultural diversity and great people, but the stories about it from folks looking in are far too negative far too often. There's an oft-used quote: "Until the lion tells his side of the story, the tale of the hunt will always glorify the hunter." The hunters keep telling tales of despair about Africa.

I was born and bred in the Motherland, and it will always have my heart. My roots are planted there even as my feet are here, and I am a proud Naija gal! I wish people who have the means would travel more and see the expanse of that great continent for themselves. Maybe then folks would stop talking about and treating Mama Africa like a bald-headed, no-edges-having stepchild with lice and gout. Maybe then we could change the conversation. But until we do, consider yourselves judged.

Rape Culture Is Real and It Sucks

 When I was a senior in college, I was trained as a mandated reporter and a workshop facilitator for a program that taught kids how to stay "safe, strong and free" from abuse. We went to grade schools in Champaign-Urbana and taught kids who were in kindergarten through fifth grade that they have a right to feel safe about their bodies. We also emphasized that their feelings about how someone touches them, including trusted adults, are ALWAYS valid. After each workshop, we invited them to come talk to us one-on-one about anything. I remember when a six-year-old divulged to me that her father touched her "down there." I tried to keep my face from falling as she spoke to me. It was the first time I had to call my supervisor and draft a report. Thankfully, her father was already in jail for it—but unfortunately, that was more of the exception than the rule.

I am judging us for needing such an important program, because we're living in a world where the cycle of sexual abuse thrives and rape culture is considered a myth by too many. There is a continuum of cultural attitudes that facilitate abuse, like those of a father who touches his daughter sexually, and it starts with seemingly trite things that include catcalling.

It is an unfortunate rite of passage for girls to be walking down the street and have a guy you've never met yell something at you. He wants to get your attention, and he will do it by jeering at you. Sometimes he's in a car at a red light. Sometimes he's at his job, which you have to walk by to get to where you're going. Other times, he's just loitering, and you happen to walk by him. Far too many of us have also experienced the negative response that can come from a guy who feels ignored or rejected when we do not seem all that flattered by his remarks: "Well, fuck you too, then!" All because we did not give him the attention he felt entitled to.

There are so many people who cannot seem to fathom how we can be so "sensitive" about something like being told we're beautiful or sexy by a random dude. When women are walking down the street in the morning/afternoon/night/ever, minding our own business, one thing we are not asking for is folks' opinions on our appearance—yes, even if you think we look amazing. People will say we should be flattered that someone found us so attractive that they were moved to yell about it. Being street-harassed is not a blue ribbon, nor does it prove you have the looks of Miss America. There is no rhyme or reason to it, and it is not special. I've walked out my house looking like "whodunnit and why" and men will still catcall. It's like some of them feel like if they don't holla at someone for a day, their "talk to a girl" muscle will atrophy and become a gummy worm.

"Hey, mama! What's your name?" and "Damn, girl! You sexy as hell!" are not, and have never been, appropriate pickup lines. Do you think my ass looks amazing in these jeans? Well, great. But you do not need to let me know, strange man. Jesus invented brains so they could be the protective chambers for our thoughts. Imagine if everything we thought, we said. Our mouths would give up the ghost from too much activity. You can shut up and keep those thoughts to yourself or tell your diary. "Dear diary, her yansh was amazing." See? Simple.

Street harassment is not flattering, because it speaks to the fact that men see our presence as an opportunity for sexual advances. In a world where most girls get catcalled before they even get their first periods, you have to admit there is a problem. Girls are being sexualized by random toads and goats on the streets and told to *smile* about it. Our bodies do not exist purely for the objectification of men, and if we cannot even go a day without being made to feel uncomfortable, how can we feel like we are safe?

I do not wake up on any day with the intention of making you happy by looking at me. So contrary to you thinking you're blessing my day with your praises, please know that you are just going to make me roll my eyes. I get that "us boy, you girl," but this is not caveman times, you are not strictly ruled by your penis, and you have free will. This mind-set is why a girl can be sent home from school to change her tank top because her principal thought her shoulders would distract her male classmates and their rampant hormones. It's as if we expect the male system to run on autopilot when it comes to arousal, and that the flooding blood to their nethers will render them unable to deal. Meanwhile, girls are told to watch how we dress and manage ourselves—and apparently every guy who can see us—so as not to disturb the boys.

Usually, when we talk about street harassment being wack as hell, men will ask, "So you mean I can't talk to any woman I see on the street? What if I am mesmerized by her and want to learn more?"

I just wonder if they realize that a random sidewalk and someone who is clearly headed elsewhere is not a good pickup situation. I mean, how many love stories begin with, "He yelled at me from his car as I was going to work?"

If you insist on meeting that lady who just stole your heart at first sight, do it openly and in a way that is not threatening. Not from behind and not sneakily. Our nerves are bad because truthfully, sometimes our lives are in danger, and some of us have past traumas that may trigger us to have a negative response to your approach. Give a woman ample space as you approach her and politely say, "Hi. I saw you and I think you're pretty/beautiful/gorgeous. I would love to take you out on a date/to the movies/for coffee. Are you interested?" If she says no, respect it and say good-bye. Don't throw a tantrum like a four-year-old who didn't get dessert for breakfast. If she says yes, give her your number so there's no pressure on her to acquiesce from fear. Who knows? Maybe she'll be on *Say Yes to the Dress* in two years. But that is not how it usually goes.

Street harassment is a problem that is annoying at minimum and that at its worst can be extremely dangerous. There are women who have been injured or even killed by men who did not like their response to their catcalling. Let's think about that: men have been so enraged by not getting positive attention from *strangers* that they have gone as far as to inflict bodily harm on them. This sense of entitlement is the crux of rape culture. Men feel entitled to the attention of women, and they have been programmed to expect that they have some sort of ownership over us. Rape culture is the prevailing attitude that women exist primarily to please men, and therefore are not equal human beings with agency over their own bodies.

Rape culture does not mean every man is a rapist. It does mean that we're surrounded by a cultural atmosphere that perpetuates and enables the harming and violation of girls and women physically, emotionally, and sexually. (Men are also victims of this toxic mind-set.) Rape culture makes it easy for people who *are* abusive to injure women and makes it hard for women to feel safe. I am judging people who don't recognize that this is another system of oppression that we live in and that it should be taken seriously. I am endlessly side-eyeing people who are not trying to be a part of the solution, because they don't even want to acknowledge that there is a problem. Women feel vulnerable, and we have more than enough reason to.

Let's talk about rape. It's a harsh, ugly word that comes with harsh, ugly visuals. Rape is a violation of someone's body. Someone is raped when they have a sexual act performed on them or are forced to perform a sexual act without their consent or against their will. It is also what happens when an adult has sexual contact with a child, because that power dynamic is so unequal that the Libra scales would break. A child *cannot* consent to having sex with an adult. IT IS RAPE. Rape is not about being horny or wanting sex. It's about rapists wanting to dominate and exert control over others whom they perceive to be weaker. It is about theft, because they're taking something that is not theirs to have, yet they feel like it belongs to them. It is about ownership, which is reinforced when the rapist is protected by law.

The majority of rapists are men. Not to be confused with "the majority of men are rapists." Let that be clear. We are not pointing the finger at each of you. But your peen brethren are the ones who are being violent toward women and girls and sometimes toward other men and boys.

One out of five girls and one in twenty boys are victims of child sexual abuse.[16]

Those kids are not just being caught up by stranger danger. They are being violated by trusted adults.

The fact that it surprised me that the father of that little girl I spoke with after the workshop is in jail for his crime of violating her is saddening. Girls and women are being violated constantly, at varying levels of severity, and we are dealing with a society that does not protect us, does not punish our violators, and sometimes even protects predators. We think of rape as the act of a boogeyman who is lurking in alleys, snatching up unsuspecting women

---

[16]This statistic is from the Crimes Against Children Research Center. https://victimsofcrime.org/media/reporting-on-child-sexual-abuse/child-sexual-abuse-statistics.

who are dressed too tawdrily like he's Dora the Explorer's twisted Swiper, just waiting behind the dumpster. But everyday people can be rapists, and 70 percent of women who are sexually assaulted are victimized by someone they know: family members, friends, neighbors, acquaintances. It's fathers, uncles, and cousins, not necessarily unfamiliar pedophiles and predatory felons. These are people who are embedded in our lives and people we trust who are hurting us. It's hard for people to grasp this, because then they'd have to admit that they live surrounded by, and may be a part of, this problem.

This is why whenever a woman says she's been raped, people will jump down her throat to disprove her. Surely she cannot have been raped by that straight-A student, or that star basketball player, or that sergeant. People rush to discredit survivors and protect perpetrators because it's easier to deny that something happened than to deal with the fact that there are predators in our midst.

Unfortunately, all this victim-blaming does is reinforce the cycle of fuckshit. A man rapes a woman, the woman speaks up about it, the woman is then vilified, the man walks. And then when other victims of sexual abuse clam up and decide not to come forward, we have the nerve to ask why. We use their years of silence as proof that they are probably making it up, and it is maddening. *Maddening.* In spite of the fact that less than 5 percent of rape allegations are found to be false, we still cast doubt on the woman who dares to assert that she was violated.

In this environment, why *would* anyone feel confident about speaking up about being sexually abused? All we'll do is revictimize them. When a woman is raped, and people ask what she did to get raped, a thousand angels do a collective *wall-slide.*[17] No one has ever asked to be raped. Did she drink too much? Sure, she

---

[17] *wall-slide*: When something happens that renders you unable to talk about your feelings, so all you can do is just slide down a wall. Think of most Lifetime movies.

might have. But it's her prerogative to drink, and it's everyone else's responsibility to know that she cannot make meaningful decisions if she's drunk or passed out. Someone who is unconscious cannot consent, and pointing the finger at her is disgusting. The questionable personal decisions we sometimes make do not excuse the bad decisions others make, especially when it comes to how they interact with us. It's like if someone is standing too close to the train tracks and I push them when the train is coming: it does not matter how foolish it was for them to stand so close to the rails. I had no right to send them falling.

The fact that when a woman is molested she's automatically asked what she was wearing is appalling. Who gives a fuck what she had on? It coulda been nothing but body paint; it makes no difference. Unless she gives consent, it is rape. You could be rocking footie pajamas, or a thong only, and you still won't be inviting someone to sexually assault you. Why? Because our bodies belong to us, and we have a right to demand that others keep their hands, peens, and whatever else to themselves. We give clothes a lot of power—too much power. No one wakes up and says, "Today, I will be forcefully penetrated. Let me put on these tiny shorts. They'll make it easier." Clothes should not determine your humanity or how much agency you are allowed to have over your own body. People say things like, "Well, if she dressed respectably, then maybe she'll be treated with respect." But people have been raped while wearing pinstriped suits. People have been raped while wearing military uniforms. People have been violated in nun's habits or burqas, which only expose their eyes. It does not matter. "Respectability" in clothing choice does not determine one's safety, because we live under a stifling system of oppression that says women's love pockets are for the taking. The idea that victims of violent crimes—whether rape at the hands of a man or murder by police who thought sagging pants makes you a criminal—asked for it is crazy. NOPE. I am not here for it.

To rub salt in the wound, sexual assault survivors have to deal with a broken process that does not get them anything resembling justice. It should be no wonder that some victims take years to come forward and others might never divulge that they were violated. People who have been raped have very little, if anything, to gain by speaking up about what happened, and they have everything to lose. They are discredited and made to feel like they're the ones on trial as their characters are assassinated. Rape is not a tool that women use to get the upper hand, because there is no winning for women. So operating from a place of disbelief when women and girls say "I've been assaulted" is hustling backwards.

Our apparent need to protect men instead of giving their victims space to share their experiences is a real shame. We don't give these women the benefit of the doubt, and in turn, we hand down no consequences to their violators. This helps continue the cycle of abuse, because lack of real punishment signals our approval. It's almost like we're giving perpetrators a silent high five, and that is awful.

Additionally, victims who speak out are often made to face their abusers over and over again, acutely triggering their trauma. There are people who are surrounded by those who would believe them and support them, and yet they still find it difficult to come forward. Imagine having to tell the story of the moment your life was split open in front of a number of people who do not have any investment in your well-being. You have to relive that devastating ordeal as strangers search your face for truth—often directly in front of the person who caused your trauma. It becomes a "he says/she says" case, and her say does not have the same weight as his say. Why? Because the voices of women aren't trusted unless men cosign, and the testimony of a woman who has been raped and violated is not enough.

The system is already stacked against women and girls, and for them to agree to experience such pain might turn out to be for naught, because the asshole who raped them will probably walk away scot-free anyway. Tens of thousands of rape kits have gone untested around the United States. It's clear that there are no fucks to give about getting women justice. So I can absolutely understand why some people never come forward or divulge their ordeal.

And what type of justice can you expect to get when the crime committed against you is fodder for jokes? When people still use rape as a punch line, how can survivors think they will be taken seriously when they tell their stories? When music artists brag about drugging and having sex with women, and those songs become hits, you realize that your trauma isn't going to be taken seriously. It took fifty (fifty!) women coming forward to accuse an entertainment icon of rape before he was finally called to the carpet. Even now, there are still people saying all those women are liars, defending him in the face of overwhelming odds. If only those apologists spent more time dedicating themselves to other shit, like not being dinglebats. If avoiding holding men accountable for despicable sexual behavior was an Olympic sport, our society would be full of Hall of Famers. There can be video of a popular musician urinating on an underage girl, yet he is still free and continuing to prosper. Rape culture gives predators the benefit of the doubt in the court of public opinion and in our actual courtrooms. There is seldom anything resembling justice for victims of sexual violence. It is preposterous and rage-inducing.

There's also the disgusting assertion that some people will loudly make that anyone who is a sex worker cannot be raped. Some people who are supposedly anti-rape will turn around and claim that if you are a prostitute, you cannot accuse anyone of rape. Apparently in such a case, if you are molested by someone who you did not give consent to, it is more "theft" than "rape" because someone just took the goods you were offering. That is not an occupational hazard; that is rape rape rape. It is rape. Someone who is forced into a sexual act without their consent was raped. It does not matter if she usually accepts money for sex. Our bodies should never be property, so to claim "theft" is to deny the human within that vessel.

Rape culture has taught people that women do not have inherent value as human beings who deserve dignity. We must earn it through being "ladylike." And when we do not fit into the scope of that conveniently vague and subjective category, the things that are done to us and our bodies are just part of what we've asked for. So a sex worker is considered at the bottom rung of the ladder and whatever violation she experiences is part of what she has brought on herself. That's foul.

No one deserves to be raped, not even someone who has committed a crime that has landed them in jail. Rape as a tool of punishment is savagery. Rape in prison is still rape, and it's still wrong, and your prison jokes are awful. Sexual assault is a crime that does not end when the perpetrator zips up their pants. It creates a cycle of shame. We have to fix these twisted ideas.

But what do we do now? With all systems of oppression, the onus on fixing it needs to be placed on the majority group, not on the group that is experiencing the violation. Just as Black people cannot fix racism, women cannot fix this rape culture. Although there are some women who help uphold this culture by spewing some of the same misogynistic garbage, they are not wholly to blame; any large-scale system of oppression will often have some of the oppressed believing its teachings. Countless women have internalized rape culture and will blame themselves for being raped or point the finger at other women who were raped and say it was their fault. They are just a part of a well-oiled machine of patriarchy. It is up to men to dismantle the douchebaggery and get things right. We're too busy teaching girls shame when we need to be teaching boys how to see women as more than vessels of sex.

At my college orientation, freshman girls had to take a class on how to avoid being raped. I truly hope the class the boys had to take was called "DO NOT RAPE ANYONE." Girls have been given tips on how to make sure they do not become victims. But when most of us are being attacked by people we know, those tips (like not rocking your headphones when you're walking at night) become wholly pointless.

The problem is not what women are wearing or how much we drink at parties. It is with boys who become men who think they are entitled to women's time, attention, and bodies. We need to teach them that they are not. When they hear "no," they should not feel like a "yes" is owed to them. Teach your sons that women exist for more than the purpose of pleasuring them. Teach boys that you take someone's humanity away when you treat their bodies like property. Teach boys to be whole human beings themselves, not just shells of machismo, with the full spectrum of emotions and the vulnerability that sometimes comes with it. They say girls are made of sugar and spice, but it seems we think boys are made of hormones and semen, because they are not held accountable for their actions or attitudes. We are told that "boys will be boys." Nonsense.

Can we stop living this lowered-expectations life when it comes to actual people who should be able to show restraint? I can hear you already protesting: "Not me; I would never rape or violate anyone. I respect women." Okay, "good guys," here's how you can help. First of all, treating a woman with respect does not make you good. It makes you someone who is doing the bare minimum. Also, when you are silent or laugh in the face of jokes or stories about women being violated, you're enabling misogyny. Speak up for us, even when we are not in the room. When your boy makes a rape joke or harasses a woman and you stand around not letting him know he's wrong, you're part of the problem. Our peers set the standards for our behavior, so when you let terrible things slide, you're saying it's okay. It's an endorsement. So be an actual good guy. Walk the walk and stand up against rape culture when you see it.

We gotta get our shit together, society. We've even got men in suits on Capitol Hill and in statehouses telling women what to do with our bodies through the law—in case you hadn't gotten the message that our bodies are not seen as our own.

This rape culture we live in tries to cut women down to size everywhere, all the time. We have to fight like Miss Sophia for people to treat our bodies with respect so that when we walk outside in the dark, we don't feel the need to carry rape whistles in order for us to trust that the men we love dearly won't hurt us.

We need to know that it is never our fault when we get raped. We deserve justice always.

Nobody Wins at the Feminism Olympics

 I remember when I told someone I might not take my husband's name when I get married. You would have thought I told them that I like to bathe in beet juice. They sneered and replied, "You and this feminism shit." I mean, I guess. The decision is about me being able to have a say about the name I want to go by for the rest of my life. I've carried the last name "Ajayi" for so long that to wake up one day, say "I do," and then drop it might feel jarring to me. I see the pros, though. Existing as a unit, along with my kids, under one common name is adorable to me. So although change scares me, I'm still open to it. I might not take his last name if it's something like "Butt," though. And that's just my personal preference. Everyone else? It's perfectly up to them what they want to do with their name after marriage.

On second thought, this IS a feminist issue for me.

Believing that people should make their own choices about their own lives is ultimately what I think it means to be a feminist.

Feminism is largely defined (in dictionaries and whatnot) as advocacy for women to have political, social, and economic equality. It is the belief that your gender should not determine your access to opportunities, nor should it mean you have fewer rights. For me, being a feminist means believing that women, and everyone, really, have the right to live life on their own terms, and that is why I define myself as such. When we strip it down to its bare definition, everyone should be a feminist.

Everyone *should* want to be a feminist, but so many people are uncomfortable with that identifier. Feminism has a bad rap (worse than Vanilla Ice's) both fairly and unfairly earned, and in all its misunderstandings, it has become more divisive than it should be. It's like the angst-ridden teenager of activism, and people just don't get its struggles. Why is that? Because it is becoming synonymous with white women and that insidious white privilege we talked about before.

The feminist movement is supposed to fight for the freedom of all women from oppression, ensuring that we're all getting the same access to care, jobs, money, and positions of power as men. But let's be real: feminism has mostly worked hard for those things for *white women*, and that is one of the main reasons why it gets its wig snatched so often.

A white woman named Dale Spender said, "Feminism has fought no wars. It has killed no opponents. It has set up no concentration camps, starved no enemies, practiced no cruelties." I am here to say, "Hey, gal. I get you, but I disagree a bit."

Feminism might not have started any wars, but it has been cruel by not equally prioritizing—and in some cases actually working against—the issues of women of color, and women who are not heterosexual, and basically any woman who isn't straight and white. It has upheld a system of white supremacy by primarily serving that group, and it has made others invisible in its battles and on its front lines. It might not be the reason for World War III, but it is culpable and complicit in how some women are still marginalized and struggling while others are uplifted as the ideal of womanhood. I understand why some women of color have deep issues with it and refuse to identify as feminists. Feminism hasn't started any wars, but its battles are mostly fought by self-righteous white women who don't even realize that their work often only benefits people like them. When the big F has not cared about your unique issues, has not fought the extra layers of oppression that nonwhite, nonstraight women face, and has undermined your own efforts at seeking equality and freedom, you are probably in no rush to put yourself under its unwelcoming umbrella. I am a feminist in spite of all this, but many of my friends identify as womanists, understandably. Like Alice Walker said: "Womanist is to feminist as purple is to lavender."

For Black women, not only do we deal with misogyny but racism adds an extra scoop of fuckedupness to the big bowl of crap we have to put up with. Have white feminists stepped up to help us address those issues? Have they used their privilege to be allies to us as we face the pain of seeing our children, men, uncles, and aunties suffer the often violent effects of racism? Or do we have to battle alone as our "friends in feminism" stand idly by? Are they fighting along with us as we endure feeling ignored, unconsidered, and exhausted from shouldering the weight of not just patriarchy but a racist patriarchy? Or are white women adding to our burdens by ostracizing us, too? What is even more ridiculous is that women of color were pioneers in the feminist movement. An early movement symbol was of a fist in a female gender icon; the fist is clearly an homage to the Black Power fist. Feminism is standing on the shoulders of giants who were Black and brown women, so for it to have evolved into something that excludes us adds insult to injury. We are rendered invisible, like we didn't pitch the tent on the feminism lawn and start the campfire our damb selves. It's so rude.

The big enemies of feminism are the institutions that continue to oppress women: Sexism, its meaner brother, Misogyny, and its evil-ass dad, The Patriarchy. We all throw darts at them. That is every woman's shared common ground, right? Yes, except that the misogyny we all experience is *also* colored by our race, sexual orientation, and gender identity. We are all marginalized at varying levels, and I'm speaking as a straight Black woman here so I can only talk about my point of view.

The misogyny that white women get looks different from ours, and our struggles aren't in the same box. They might be called "bitch," but we get called "nigger bitch." They might make 77 cents for every dollar that a white man makes on the job, but a Black woman gets only 64 cents out of that white man's dollar. What is feminism doing to ensure us equity, not just equality? I'm not sure, but certainly many Black women feel like we don't have a seat at the table.

Our struggles are surely not the same, and it isn't just in the way the rest of the world treats us, but also in how issues are prioritized within mainstream feminism itself. They say we're all on the same team, but they've made themselves the starting lineup, only bringing us in when the clock is winding down at the end of the fourth quarter. We have the right to feel like we're not playing the same game at all.

When has The Movement itself ever centered the issues of Black and brown women specifically? What has feminism done for us lately (ooh-ooh-ooh-ooh yeah)? Who has feminism advanced in the last ten, twenty, or fifty years? Feminists in comedy? Feminists in media? Feminists who run shit? White women. So again, why should women of color be so quick to raise their hands enthusiastically about being feminists?

Over the years, white feminists have removed Black women from the narrative of the movement. How many movies about women fighting for the right to vote include women of color? It's as if we weren't on those front lines, too. Our contributions are erased time and time again, but white feminists want all of us to fall under the same tag. They don't understand how women who are actively doing anti-misogyny work in their professional and personal lives could shirk the word "feminism." It's like being in a club that skips over your name when it's time for roll call—you will feel like more of an observer than a part of the group. It's like we can't sit with them because on Wednesdays they wear pink, but they kept all the pink sweaters for themselves. White feminism has bred far too many mean girls who think they are fighting for all women but who are really fighting just for the ones who look like them.

Let's face it: at the intersection of racism and sexism is white women's privilege, and while some feel like they're dismantling one system, they're often upholding another. In a world that does a piss-poor job of protecting all women and keeping us safe, when society does choose to fight for women, it's usually for white women only. The rest of us can go fend for ourselves because "Strong Black Woman" and "Fiery Latina Woman" are tropes used to dehumanize us, excusing the bad treatment we receive. Some women are treated like fine china, while the rest of us are disposable plates that you reuse because you're too cheap to buy more. Because we can handle it, right?

Too often feminists are fighting for women to live in a way that mirrors their own lives. As in, if you're in middle America in middle management, you want other women to have your life. You're not Muslim? You fight for women to not have to cover their heads as they worship. The assumption that women in hijabs are less enlightened or empowered than those rocking daisy dukes is arrogant at best. Feminism should fight for all women to have the right to live as they choose, not for all women to live the same exact lives like we're all in some sort of Sims game.

Privilege is also in play when white women are portrayed as damsels in distress while the rest of us are meant to fend for ourselves. It is why missing blond girls get news coverage and little brown girls in the same situation rarely get attention. It is why people are quick to throw the words "bullying" and "shaming" at critiques of white women, but the rest of us are just being "corrected." And those very white women who quickly come to the defense of those who look like them are often nowhere to be found when Black and brown women are being treated like wretches. This ego-driven fragility is why some people have reduced feminism to a puddle of white women's tears, and yet they will scream, "Aren't we all feminists?"

The feminist movement has sucked at being truly intersectional. It has neglected to address the struggles of women who are not straight, white, Christian (or sometimes Jewish), and cisgender (identifying as the gender that corresponds to the body you were born with). A woman who is Black, trans, or Muslim won't be represented fairly and completely in the fight for equality. Yet even with all these glaring issues, white women have claimed themselves the authority on feminism, and that is insulting. When feminism fights for the concerns of white women and not *all* women, it implies that white women epitomize femininity, which offends me. Not only does it make white-cis-Christian the default of femininity; it implies that other women have to live *up to* these narrow criteria. It assumes that everyone's feminism and idea of empowerment needs to be identical to theirs. Going back to the example of Muslim women who wear hijab: for many, the hijab is worn with a sense of pride. But some Christian feminists will choose to pity them, wondering how they can be liberated from their polyester and silk prisons. *Who asked you?* Who told you they're all feeling oppressed? We are not fighting for sameness in life. We're fighting for equality. We are fighting for choice.

The pressure to fit the increasingly rigid standards for being considered a feminist can be too much. It's like we're in a feminism competition, and the person who can prove they're the most feminist wins an island. I'm good and tired of people having to prove their feminism, as if there's some sort of entry exam that folks need to pass before they use the label. Setting all these criteria cannot be useful for progress, because all it does is encourage us to fight about whether we're worthy of a term that is supposed to encourage freedom. It's actually pretty counterproductive. It's a waste of time, and it's an exercise in elitism. Feminism is not some exclusive clubhouse where you have to dress a certain way and use a certain password to be allowed in. It is not a way to make women measure their lives against other women's lives. And it certainly is not about following rules.

"Real feminists don't wear heels." (They're oppressive and were created by men.) "Real feminists don't wear short skirts." (They open you up to being objectified.) "Real feminists shun plastic surgery." (Patriarchy has made you hate your body and face.) "Real women don't twerk." (Dancing sexualizes your body.) Well shit, "real" feminists sound boring, prudish, and plain as hell. Can they relax a bit?

Beyoncé has stood in front of fifteen-foot electric signs that say "FEMINIST" and identified herself as such. Yet there are multiple articles asking whether she is *really* a feminist. Since she chooses to use her beauty in her art, has a penchant for not wearing pants, and happens to be a woman of color, her feminism is constantly being called on the carpet. Every time someone writes an "Is Beyoncé Really a Feminist?" article, an angel gets a paper cut. This is absurd to me. Because until white feminists give you the stamp of approval, you're not really a feminist yet. How many articles have been written questioning Madonna's feminism? Surely far fewer than those questioning Bey's.

Of course feminism doesn't mean that we're all above critique, but the backlash should not be about how feminist someone is or is not. A woman who chooses to have Botox or plastic surgery or a bad weave, or who changes her appearance in any way she chooses, is no less of a feminist than anyone else. Sure, I might tell you that I wish you had kept your old face and that weave you got looks like a squirrel died on your scalp. However, I *can't* tell you that you're less committed to the equality struggle because of it. If feminism means we cannot judge the choices other women make, then I pretty much suck at it. (Because I judge everyone equally. I even wrote a book about it!) But someone's decisions about their own life doesn't mean I revoke their Feminism Clubhouse membership. Besides, they make the best mac and cheese, and I'd miss it at our annual potluck. Chantay, you stay.

Feminism is an ideology that is supposed to promote freedom from limits. A housewife who chooses to be one because it's what she wants is no less a feminist than a woman who works because she wants to make her own money. That stripper who is happy doing something brash for cash might be no less a feminist than the CEO. Too many people have a cramped idea of what feminism is, and all it does is marginalize women and discourage more of us from using that label.

The people who judge the "You can do it"-ness of those who choose to take their husband's name are part of the patriarchy they fear. Womanhood should be defined by each person for herself, because we are not all the same, and there's no one way we can define it as a group. If someone else's happy looks like them being a wife who takes her husband's name, that's perfectly fine. Ridiculing someone who chooses to be traditional in her daily life is just as harmful as expecting all women to be bad at math. It's too bad that people have to be shamed about whatever their choices are, or have their feminism questioned because they do not conform to a limited set of criteria.

Ideology can go to hell when the people who practice it consider themselves the gatekeepers, always wanting to play "Feminism Olympics: Prove Your Worth."

Then there are people who think that feminism—and I mean the base "equality for all" feminism I defined at the beginning of this chapter—is not even needed, and I'd like to offer them a hoe (as in the instrument, not the pejorative term for women) to scoop up all the bullshit they've surrounded themselves with. These people live in a dreamland that exists only in their heads where women are already equal. They think because they have that one boss who is a woman, we've made enough progress. They know that one person who didn't take her husband's last name, and he doesn't even care! We can pack it in!

Those people are lying to themselves, but they're not as bad as the people who hear the word "feminist" and think of a caricature version of the bra-burning man-hater whose purpose is to tear down all men. (Most feminists I know love our bras for keeping our nipples from telling everyone the weather.)

Way too many people have come to think of feminism as the belief system of hating or emasculating men. Misandry is not feminism, and if an eye for an eye makes the world go blind, we will all need service dogs if we try to fight hate with more hate. Wanting equal rights for women is not synonymous with wanting fewer rights for men, just like me having the option of ordering a salad doesn't mean you're not allowed to order red meat. The fight for equality on any front does not equate to the oppression of the oppressors. Thinking that feminism's critiques of the patriarchy are somehow threatening to men as a whole is exactly why it is necessary. Feminism exists to level the playing field, because things are anything but fair, because patriarchy (and racism) permeates every part of our existence, and everyone who isn't a straight white man suffers for it.

We need feminism because men won't get the hell out our wombs. Politicians have made it their business to control how women deal with their bodies. If men had to be pregnant and go through childbirth, the human race would have gone extinct a long time ago, old low-tolerance-for-pain-having asses. Men catch one little cold and act like they're dying from the plague, but then they want to control whether we get abortions or not? Some of them are bold enough to tell us we can't even get them in cases of rape and incest. The unmitigated gall!

We need feminism because women can't just be who they are without being qualified and represented by their relationship to men. Our obituaries still start by defining us by who we were married to, even when we leave a legacy of our own accomplishments.

We need feminism because people believe that married women are the property of their husbands, and therefore they cannot be raped by them. It does not help that the Bible says wives should be led by their husbands, which some people have taken to mean "obey like a dog and let him do what he wants." NOPE.

We need feminism because women are still underrepresented in almost every field that is not nursing or teaching. In Congress, in technology, and in executive positions in all industries, we don't see ourselves enough. There are conferences that talk about women's issues where the panelists and speakers onstage are all men. You know what makes no sense? A bunch of penises making choices for vaginas. That's like interviewing a turtle on the struggles of being a dolphin.

We need feminism because dolls are for girls and trucks are for boys. And girls wear pink and boys wear blue. And women cook and men fix things. And women are emotional and men should never cry. And women get PMS so they should not lead companies. These are prevailing (and simplistic) attitudes that show how basic we are with these gender binaries we enforce.

We need feminism because men are still getting high-fived for being present in their children's lives. People congratulate men who "babysit" their own kids. How the hell are you babysitting a child that you made? That is called *parenting*. You do not get a cookie for changing your kid's diaper, people! This comes as part of the territory, but it is so embedded in us to think it is the job of women that even those of us who are progressive can't help but be impressed by a father who spends as much time taking care of his kids as mothers do. We need feminism like the desert needs rain and like my dry scalp needs jojoba oil. These flakes are as real as the oppression of women; both must be demolished.

I just want women to be able to thrive, and my form of feminism is pretty simple: I do what I want to do and know I have the right. I gladly wear bras, and the only time I won't shave my legs is in the wintertime, because I'm skinny and I need the extra fur for warmth. I would submit to a man if I trusted that he could lead me. Submission is not synonymous with obedience, and I'm undecided about taking my husband's name when I get married. This is my feminism, hear me purr!

Let's stop administering the Feminism Membership Quiz, because all it's doing is ostracizing people and making them feel unwelcome in a movement that is supposed to be about inclusion. White women, include women of color in your agenda as you fight for equality. Don't leave us behind and then only call on us when you need our numbers. Feminism is for all of us, so fight for us. Don't just use your power and voices when it affects someone who looks like you.

You know why we still need feminism? Because "slut," "whore," "hoe," and "bitch" are still so embedded in our lingo to denigrate women. We need to defeminize them. I want to live in a world where these words no longer have an automatic connotation to women and girls. Because let's be ULTRAREAL. Men will dip their Groupon peens everywhere and get high fives from their counterparts. Those ones embody that flimsy-ass definition of "hoe." And bitchassness knows no chromosome, sees no genitals, and crosses boundaries of gender identity. This is what equality looks like.

By the way, fellas, you can be feminists, too. We need more of you to say you are. That's sexy. I mean, don't say you are just to make it a pickup line. Actually believe it. Hey, boo. Call me sometime, with your respectful ass.

Become a CEO of a Fortune 500 company. Stay at home and raise your children. Keep the name you've always had. Change your name to your husband's. Hyphenate it. Create a new name for your family. Refuse to cook because you hate it. Cook every single day. Have some big-headed children. Don't have any kids. Be a sex worker. Be a stripper. Be an accountant. Be Martha Stewart.

Be Oprah. Be Jennifer the Random. Wear short shorts. Wear a cloak. Wear heels. Wear flats. Whatever it is you are doing right now, you are a feminist if that is what you want to be doing. If you are free to make your own choices, and think that other women should also have that freedom, you are a feminist. If you believe that everyone should be on equal footing, no matter what gender they claim or do not claim, you are a feminist. It is that simple.

Homophobia Is Geigh

 I went to a restaurant with one of my guy friends, and our server (a guy) told my friend his shirt was nice. He then quickly added, "Not that I'm gay or anything," as a statement of record. He wanted us to make sure we knew it, because when he came back, he said it again. "That's a really nice shirt. No homo."

When did being gay start including attraction to shirts? Because if that is true, I need to figure out some things about myself and how I feel about shoes. I wanted to tell him to relax—pointing out that another man's shirt is nice does not make implications about the type of person you'd like to end up in bed with. It's like being all "OMG, I love chicken. Not that I'm Black or anything." DAFUQ? What does that have to do with the price of beads in Togo?

We heteros were, and often still are, very pressed to ensure that we aren't confused with members of the LGBTQ community. Our haste to accompany any compliment we give to someone of the same gender with a qualifier to remind people that we are not gay is kinda homophobic. Well, not kinda. It is. I'm judging us for that and for other ways we thrive at being unreasonable toward people who identify or present as lesbian, gay, bisexual, trans, queer, or gender-nonconforming. "No homo" and its cousins are proof that we cannot have nice things, like the end of anti-gay bigotry.

Being homophobic does not mean you actively hate and wish harm on people who are gay. Nah. Homophobia doesn't always look like yelling out slurs or cutting off your friend who just came out the closet. It's in the fact that we're so uncomfortable with people's private sexuality that we casually and hurtfully distance ourselves from it as much as we can. It is pervasive and it is high-level petty, but most important, it is dangerous.

Why do people care who someone else loves or sleeps with as long as all are consenting adults? The way some people take homosexuality as a personal affront will never cease to amaze me. The way hateful shrews carry on and on about gay people, you'd think there's some secret Make Everyone Gay Council that runs into every house where straights reside just to transform their curtains into rainbow satin. Some people are so chafed about it that you'd think they were being forced to have sex with someone they don't want to in their own home as a result of the existence of gay people.

Part of this is because we carry stereotypical ideas of what the LGBTQ community is like and we use them to ridicule and disparage the entire group. Folks thinking all gay men are neck-swerving, shrill pink tutu wearers, while gay women are butch lumbersexuals with bad haircuts. Sure, some might fit into these stereotypical descriptions, but not all. Not even most. And what's so scary or negative about those things anyway? But there is no nuance in hate, and clichés don't have time for gradients.

You ask a homophobe why they are against homosexuality and one of the things they will tell you is, "It isn't natural."

How do they know that homosexuality isn't of nature? Were they there when all of this was being made, so that they know what everyone's loins are supposed to like or not like? Were you shooting at Creation Gym?

The idea that a large group of people being romantically attracted to someone of the same gender goes against nature is not only presumptuous but hella offensive. You're telling countless people that their feelings are abnormal, so you're basically thinking they're perverse. This idea usually comes with the addition that man and woman is the only true couple because their combination keeps humanity going. No, a same-sex couple cannot conceive with each other, but procreation is not the only point of marriage and couplehood. If that's the case, should a man or woman who has fertility issues be barred from marrying? Should older people (who are past birthing age) be shut down from saying "I do?" What about people who do not want children by choice? Did they waste marriage-license ink? Besides, you know what isn't from nature? High-fructose corn syrup, and we clearly don't care about that as we sip all our sodas and whatnot. Someone's feelings toward someone else based on whether they pee standing or sitting is way more natural than a lot of other things we do. Like running marathons. *Why are you putting your bodies through that?* Don't listen to me, though. I really think marathoners are tools of propaganda, and I don't believe in that ministry.

When the "it's not natural" crowd is told to shut the whole entire fuck up, the "gay people are responsible for our loose morals" choir wakes up from their nap. The Archie Bunkers of the world think where there are gay people, there's some illicit, sexually deviant, freak-nasty activity going on. If only. That would make my life way more memorable as I live-tweet my neighborhood's exploits. I live near Boystown in Chicago. There are rainbow flag poles everywhere, but you'd be so disappointed by how little nakedness and live porn I see. I take a stroll in the neighborhood and I don't see errant penises high-fiving each other, not even at nighttime. They really ought to do something about that. Where are the men in lime-green thongs standing on the corner on a random Wednesday and slapping each other on the ass as they do all types of crude movements with their pelvises? There's a noticeable lack of brothels and harems where I live, too. I have been hoodwinked and bamboozled. Where are the gay women who can magically turn any woman they pass by into a raving lesbian? This is what the travel guide said, and I don't see any of it. Can I get a refund? Who do I write a letter to?

Look, jerkwads. I'm pretty sure that society's morals don't need the help of gay people to get looser. Also, what do loose morals look like? If it is adults who know what they want, go for it, and keep that shit consensual, that's not "loose." That is being *open*. A world full of prudes is a global Utah, and I don't want us to all have to go through that.

LGBT does not stand for "Let's Get Busy Tonight," and there isn't a contest to see who amongst them can have sex with the most people. If you think gay people are more sexually free, then you should be jealous, not angry. I wouldn't attribute freakiness to everyone under the umbrella, though. That's like saying everyone who is straight is a lover of missionary only. That's so vanilla, but if that's what you love, I'm not hating on it. I'm just suggesting you might wanna get your sexual cookies up.

Being gay is not synonymous with being promiscuous, BUT if someone chooses to sleep with *every adult on earth*, that's fine as long as it's consensual and safe. Besides, the Gaytown of your dreams is only close to happening on Pride weekend, and even then it's pretty tame. Lower your expectations. I've been told by good gays in my life that there is no Gay Agenda that is plotting to turn society into one giant orgy (or a reenactment of the terrible and pointless movie *Eyes Wide Shut*). Relax your assholes, asshole straights.

The most common justification for anti-gay discrimination is based on holy books, which people use to threaten folks with hellfire and brimstone. Religion has certainly been the judge, jury, and bailiff of rampant homophobia. One of the most common arguments that people trot out, like a prejudiced prizewinning puppy, is that homosexuality is immoral because Leviticus 18:22 says, "You shall not lie with a male as one lies with a female; it is an abomination."

The book of Leviticus considers seventy-six things to be sins, including eating shellfish and pork. Nothing will come between me and my shrimp and lobster. I don't eat bacon, but I bet some of you would rather risk the fires of hell than to stop eating that pork. Swine ain't mine, but it is listed in the same chapter where gay ain't the way. However, many people who argue against homosexuality citing this won't give up their pig chew. Let me find out that there are levels to this abomination thing.

Leviticus also considers letting your hair look rough (10:6), wearing two different materials in one outfit (19:19), and drinking alcohol in holy places (10:9) to be punishable offenses. A Catholic priest rocking a polyester-and-wool robe who just heard a criminal confession but stays mum about it and takes Communion with his hair all ruffled would get an express ticket to the depths of damnation, according to the holy book.

The "don't lie with a male" passage is what folks are using to tell people why they shouldn't love someone who is the same gender as them? That petty, nitpicky verse in the Bible? I'm judging you, and you need more people.

If you're going to ignore the rest of those laws, but you're holding on to Leviticus 18:22 like an Unbreakable Vow from the Harry Potter stories, then you're being hypocritical. Let me see you out here in these streets at Red Lobster's Endless Shrimp event talking about how you can't support gay marriage. May your waitress withhold the rest of the Cheddar Bay biscuits from you, so that all you can do is smell their buttery delicious goodness all around you, making them so close yet so very far. May your stomach growl in protest. It's so phony.

Divorce is also against the rules, so if you're as straight as a ruler but you married that person who really didn't turn out to be good for you, you better stay, or you might be on the express train to Satan's basement resort.

Oh, and do you have any tattoos? Because that's not allowed either (19:28).

The Bible also endorses polygamy, yet that's illegal in the United States. It is legal in more than forty-eight other countries. There is no consistency in our rule-following, therefore, there should be no hard-and-fast rule that people hold on to regarding homosexuality. Sure, there might be no chapter in the Bible on Adam and Steve. Maybe Eve and Lillian convinced them it'll be in the next edition. We don't even know! All I want people to realize is that using the Good Book as a prop in their homophobia is duplicitous. People are screaming about Sodom and Gomorrah, and I'm asking them to sit down and get it together. If we want to use the Good Book to justify hate, and Jesus preached love, at what point do we stop to reconcile *that* major discrepancy? It just doesn't line up.

On June 28, 2015, marriage equality finally became the law of the land in the United States, and love won. The Supreme Court ruled that it was unconstitutional to prevent a couple from getting married and receiving legal benefits. FINALLY.

Needless to say, not everyone was celebrating, and you would think some people were given a thousand paper cuts the moment the Supreme Court said that love is love and it doesn't need to come in the form of woman and man to be recognized by law. People cried foul as if their light bill would go up now that two people of the same gender can get married. Nothing about the lives of people who don't identify as card-carrying LGBTQ community members will change—well, besides one thing. For those of us with friends and family who are attracted to or got that agape love for someone of the same gender as them, we now get to go to their awesome love parties. Amazing weddings that you're not invited to. So sit your scowling ass at home where you get to protect your heterosexuality. That way, you won't catch THE GEIGH, nor miss out on whatever blessing you think you get for being closed-minded and not supporting love.

I think everyone should have the right to legally tie themselves to whoever they want to. The ability to be pissed when you wake up to the same person's cobweb breath every day should be for everyone. It is about time we have marriage equality in the United States. We're only decades behind other countries, like Canada, our hat. THIS is what equality looks like, and I am glad for it! Love for all, dambit!

People are too busy sobbing crocodile tears for the sudden demise of the sanctity of marriage, which is a prospering myth. We straights haven't held the institution in too high a regard, so to say marriage equality threatens the institution is disingenuous. If marriage was as sacred as folks love to claim, then half of them would not end in divorce. Also, thirty million Americans would not be signed up for a website dedicated to making cheating on their legal spouses easier by connecting them to potential side chicks and side dudes. Top politicians were discovered as users of the site. People who tout Christian values as their platform and Jesus Christ as their Lord and savior were plenty on the site. Yet gay people are being blamed for ruining the sanctity of marriage? Get outta here with that.

I called good sense and asked if it was coming back soon, and it told me not to hold my breath. To add to the absurdity, many of those who are yelling about the sanctity of marriage are married men who are so far in the closet that there's a lion and a witch by their favorite wing tips. Their wardrobe of denial is so deep, it can get you to Narnia. How many conservative, publicly and boldly homophobic male politicians have been found to have side dudes? More than we can count. They're usually outed through some scandal involving a young man who is half their age and using them as sugar daddies. I howl to the blue corn moon each time, cackling in glee.

So again, what is so holy about "traditional" matrimony? Not a damb thing. Straight marriage has cracks that are so large people fall through them and don't know how to get out, so we might as well give gay marriage a chance. They can't fuck it up as much as we already have.

But let me guess: now everyone will be confused about who and what they want. Now that there are so many options, what will people do? Will they marry animals next? Yes, because preferring a certain type of human genitals means you are totally ready to jump to bestiality. Everything is stupid and nothing makes sense. I am embarrassed for the levels of idiocy that people stoop to. *But what about the children?* They will be fine, too. They will grow up and decide for themselves if they are attracted to people with penises or vaginas. They will hopefully learn that what is important is that they make their own healthy choices and that they're happy. Stop hiding behind children, because they come out pure, and we teach them hate.

And straight men, please know that all gay men don't want you. I promise. You assume that being gay means you ain't got no standards. I am pretty sure that they have requirements for interest in a person beyond the requirement that they have a penis. Many of them wouldn't even freak you with someone *else's* penis, so you can relax, bros. Some of you really assume that you're better catches than you are. There is no Council of Gay Men in existence that plots how to prey on straight men and turn them out. *Or is there?*

If you're not a fan of homosexuality, then don't be a homosexual. If you don't support gay marriage, then don't get gay-married. Stick to straight marriage. If you think being gay is wack, then don't be gay. That's about it. Everything else, you can shut the hell up about. What you should also do while shutting up is not be a prejudiced jackass to people who do not identify as the same sexual orientation as you. And stop saying something is "gay" as a way to denigrate it and cut it down to size. That is dumb, everyone!

People are being ostracized from their families, friends, and communities for being gay. Lesbian, gay, and queer youth have higher rates of suicide than their straight peers because they are living in a world that tells them they are defective in some way. Trans men and women are being killed without consequence because of ignorance that is so atrocious that people fear their very existence. Anti-LGBTQ beliefs are not just a nuisance; they are deadly. Until we deal with them, talk about them, and commit ourselves to no longer excusing them, we will continue to endorse the deaths of people who dare to feel love that cannot be placed in the boy-girl, man-woman, or gender binary box.

People in the LGBTQ community are not the only ones who lose because of homophobia. We all suffer for it, because society's greatest skill is othering people and oppressing them, and one type of bigotry only perpetuates the presence of other kinds. Accepting homophobia in society says that it is okay for hate to fly freely. It also tells a large proportion of the population that they are not good enough to exist without disapproval, disdain, and even violence. It hollers to the abyss that who you love can make *you* unworthy of love, and that's heartbreaking. We gotta get our shit together, man.

#FixItJesus #BindItBuddha #AmendItAllah

 I am a lifelong Christian, and ever since I can remember, I've rocked a gold cross around my neck. It's sort of a faith-based security blanket for me. I was raised in a family that was held up by a pious grandmother who woke every morning at 3:00 a.m. to pray. She was a priestess in her church, and she did *not* play with her God. If you ever slept with Grandma in her bed, you'd be so mad when she woke you with her passionate whispers in the middle of the night, but you had to deal, because nothing was going to come between her and her supplication. *Amen, saints?* Yes.

To this day, I am a firm believer that her prayers cover me. I feel like God listened to her for real. Maybe it's because we went to church services that were so lengthy, God was probably like, "Look, I get it. I love you, too. Go home already." We'd be there so long we had to pack a picnic basket full of snacks so our stomachs wouldn't start speaking in tongues in the middle of the service. I really got some good naps in those services, too. REM sleep in a pew is pretty comforting as long as you have a shoulder to drool on. Good times.

When Grandma died, the sisters of her church insisted that they dress her for the funeral themselves, not some mortician. They figured all those hours spent in worship deserved some VIP treatment. I miss her dearly.

I believe in God, Jesus Christ, and angels, and I'm just getting over my fear of the dark because I've always been afraid I'd see a ghost one day. Don't judge me. Okay fine, judge away.

Anyway, I read my Bible every day (on my phone app, because: technology). I can quote my favorite Psalms (especially 91: "he who dwells in the secret place of the Most High shall abide under the shadow of the Almighty"). I feel like I am a product of God's grace. My point is, I love Jesus, and Jesus loves me, too, as this little light of mine shines. I am a person of faith, and it is an important part of my life. However, being a person of faith has not stopped me from being critical of religion. I am in it and I am of it, but I side-eye it from time to time. Why? Because religion has been one of the most powerful and often detrimental institutions in our world, and its abuse has been responsible for much of the hurt we experience. This is why I must judge us, for using religion as a tool of mass control, discrimination, oppression, and hate-mongering for so long.

You know one of the most ridiculous things about super-religious people? Some of us have the nerve to think that our religion is the one that's "right," or better than everyone else's. Whether we're Muslim, Christian, or Jewish, our faiths follow most of the same tenets: Do good. Love your neighbor. Pray to a higher power. Don't be Satan's minion. In one way or another, we all also believe in some magical, floating being (posse optional) and some rules that attempt to teach us how to be better people, so that we can get into an ideal place where the sun shines all the time and your shoes will never hurt your feet; I call that place heaven/nirvana/Idris Elba's bedroom . . . Pick whatever works for you.

So the fact that we think OUR magical floating being with special powers and great hair is more valid than the next person's is absurd. People be all: "OMG! Prophet Muhammad was NOT real. Jesus Christ was, though."

Okay, how do you figure? How can you prove one and disprove another, when they're basically different forms of the same symbol? Our hypocrisy is so real outchea! The only deity I will make fun of is whoever Scientologists worship, because they broke the mold with that alien they pray to. I'm the worst. I am part of the problem. Always.

We will even invoke history to try to disprove that someone else's magical being ever existed. Unfortunately, historical accuracy only matters when you're not looking in the mirror, because (white) Christians swear up and down that Jesus was a white man with blond hair and blue eyes. Didn't the Bible say he had hair of wool? Maybe he was rocking a Jew-fro, since he was actually Jewish. How did y'all come up with this Jesus who has hair that's been flat-ironed so straight, I'm left wondering what anti-frizz spray he used? Was that how he used the myrrh oil the wise men brought him on his birthday?

Truthful representation only seems to count when it benefits the people who want to use Jesus as their mascot. (I prefer my Jesus with an afro, by the way.) The fact that most of the imagery of Jesus is of him being fair-skinned and blue-eyed with straight hair is kinda racist. The widespread use of White Jesus has helped white people uphold racist doctrines as they insist that the holiest man ever to walk this planet was one of their ancestors. It makes it easier to justify oppressing people who look different when you can say Christ was just like you—history, logic, and accuracy be dambed. These, apparently, are the times when people take the Bible with a grain of salt. Sure, the Good Book actually gives a physical description of the Son of Man, but why pay attention to that when folks can use him as an enabler of their oppressive shenanigans?

Maybe that's why Islamophobia has been a thing amongst powerful Christians over time. Could it be because the Prophet Muhammad is accepted to be a brown man? I'm just saying, because there is a far-too-pervasive idea that Islam looks like terrorists in turbans. Sure, there are a handful of people, out of a *billion* who practice Islam, who might wage war and jihad in the name of Allah, but what about the millions of people who have committed crimes and identify as Christians? We don't accept them as representing God and Jesus Christ when they do it. Come on, Christians!

We have used our beliefs and the name of our specific magical floating being to behave like dust buckets, therefore defeating the purpose of following a religion to begin with. If the goal of believing in a higher power is to show us that we are all connected, we are all here for a reason, and we are all part of something greater than us, then why do we use our holy books to justify hate? We have created systems of persecution based on passages in the Bible and Qur'an. We have started wars in the name of Jesus and Muhammad, as if they sent us on a mission to ruin everything nice. We've sat in the ivory towers of our religions and used these doctrines to kill millions of people over centuries, all around the world, and that is an everlasting shame.

We proudly wear our religious identities on our sleeves and timelines, shouting them from rooftops and Facebook posts as loudly as we can, condemning those who don't believe as we do. Being a person of faith should be less about talking, and more about action, specifically: living a life based on love. We are too busy saying what Christianity is to actually live the principles that instruct us to serve humankind and treat each other with compassion. I cannot speak deeply on Islam, Judaism, or all the other religions that I am not a part of and have not studied, so I'll lob most of my critique here at Christianity. I throw most of my side-eyes here at my fellow "Christ followers" because I've seen how we operate up close and personal, and sometimes, it's not pretty.

There are more than seven billion people on this earth, and it would be silly if we all believed in the same things, the same doctrines, or the same God. We can't even get everyone to agree that the sky is blue. It is okay for us to diverge in our faiths (or lack thereof), but respecting our differences seems to be too much for some people. Christians have sent missionaries to indigenous societies to convert them because, again, their Jesus and their God are the only ones they think are valid. Surely, people who have had their own deities for centuries must be grateful to be told how wrong they've been doing it. And while they're there, those who came to "save" them might have destroyed cities and killed innocent people, and then forced the rest to bow to their will. Things fall apart (shout-out to Chinua Achebe!) because Christians can't just worry about themselves and instead want everyone to join their club. Joseph's stepson gotta take the wheel, be a fence, and hold my stubborn mule. He can be MY (and your) Christ and savior, but why do we need to force Him down everyone else's throats? It is appalling how people can eradicate entire cultures because: different.

Oppression and religion are not supposed to go hand in hand, but here we are leaning on holy books to denigrate groups of people and do all types of hateful things, like decimate their cultures. How does that line up with any of Christ's doctrines? Jesus might have told you to evangelize His word, but He surely ain't ask you to kill innocent people in His name. He didn't tell you to go around the world using His name to subjugate people of color and uphold white supremacy. Jesus was probably a man of color Himself! Come on, Saints and Aints.

Christianity has been used to persecute anyone who is not a straight white man, so I guess it makes sense that the Jesus used to represent it would be Aryan-nation proper. Not only is Christianity often a tool of abuse of Black and brown people, but it also helps perpetuate the denigration of gay people and women. The hypocrisy of Bible-thumping is in its selective attention to certain things while ignoring other parts just for the sake of supporting your argument. The Old Testament, especially, has been used to defend and enable homophobia, as if that same section isn't full of rules that most of us do not pay attention to (*see*: chapter 12).

The book of Genesis says that we were all created in God's image, so the idea that God could be a woman is comforting. There's something incredibly powerful in imagining and settling in the possibility that God is a SHE. Yet people are so quick to reject the idea that God could be a woman, it's mind-boggling. We are made in God's image, right? So what makes you think the only image of US—all humanity—is as a man? Especially since women are the vessels that bring forth more life. If we are a reflection of God, then every time we look at each other, we would see Him/Her/Them, no? Yes.

There's power in believing that there's God in each of us, because if we are made in His/Her/Their image, then aren't we all like good Horcruxes for God, because a piece of Them is in us? I mean, I think so. Man as the default representation of God is a patriarchal idea and has been used to shape how society treats women.

Yep, religion's role in sexism cannot be overlooked. Misogyny in religion is deeper than the flood Noah had to row through on his ark. Christianity's story of creation says women came second, so treating us like second-class citizens is engrained into the values of billions of people around the world. We've had a bad rap sheet since the beginning of time: the first sin was committed by woman (Eve), and she convinced man (Adam) to disobey God, so the things that women uniquely suffer from are said to be direct punishment for that. We were condemned to pain in childbirth, Aunt Flo, and to be ruled by men. It's not our fault that Adam didn't know how to make decisions for himself. In fact, if we were able to trick Adam into eating the forbidden fruit, why should he be trusted to lead us? NAWL. He couldn't lead a Skype meeting.

Chauvinism in biblical texts has justified laws that have led to the persistence of subservience of women to men. The Bible actually sanctions women being property, and too many societal norms have been informed and justified by this view. A wife is told to submit to her husband because he's the head of the house, but submission is not blind obedience. People interpret things differently, but the idea of submission as ownership is dangerous. It affects how women get to exercise their own agency in the confines of their marriage. Some women stay in abusive marriages because they are living the submission doctrine, and some have even submitted their lives at the hands of abusive husbands who went one punch too far, or picked up a knife, or a gun.

I definitely struggle with how the Old Testament, especially, represents women as inferior, and I struggle with how we are told that we are still paying for Eve's mistake. The Bible preaches forgiveness, but the way these cramps are set up, somebody up there is still mad at us for Eve. The sexism in the Holy Manual goes long, and it's difficult to be a Christian feminist and grapple with that. Ultimately, we attempt to make ourselves feel better by saying: the Bible is man-written, and as with all things manmade, it's flawed.

Speaking of men being faulty in religion, some of the people we've put in elevated positions to speak with God's authority are liars and cheats. Word on these holy streets is: "It is easier for a camel to go through the eye of a needle, than for a rich man to enter the kingdom of God." Yet we're playing "follow the leader" behind folks who are guiding us toward all types of dens of iniquity with greed and wealth built using the name of the Father, the Son, and the Holy Spirit.

Men (and women) of God do not need to be poor, desolate, or without sin to be of service. Preachers, pastors, and prophets aren't perfect. They are regular people who answered the call to spread the gospel, and their position lends them the ears of sinners who want to be saints. It behooves them to be more intentional with their actions and more principled than the average person. Yet we have absurdly named pastors who are asking their congregations to donate and fundraise $65 million in order to get "the church" a new, state-of-the-art private jet so they can comfortably "spread their ministry" around the world.

Are travel agents unable to get you tickets to go wherever you need to, Minister? Maybe Kayak and Expedia are blocked on the church Wi-Fi network. A man of God spending $65 million on a plane better not have *anyone* in his flock struggling to make ends meet. If you are able to make that ask of your people, they better not be people living paycheck to paycheck or wondering where their next meal is coming from. We have pimps on the pulpit preaching pride to impoverished paupers they promised to protect. CAN I GET AN AMEN FOR THAT ALLITERATION?

If the prosperity of megachurches was parallel to the prosperity of the people in the community they were in, there would be less to judge them for. But what is the point of a million-dollar mansion surrounded by shacks? What is the point of a billionaire whose closest friends are destitute?

Far too many pastors are exploiting the very people they should be helping, and all they do is tell them, "This is what Jesus wants. This is His will." How about NO, with your greedy ass? They are the worst PR reps for Jesus ever. Churching has become a business, and the distrust of it has been well earned.

There are megachurches with hundred-million-dollar budgets, and they are operating as nonprofit organizations, escaping the grubby hands of the IRS by not having to pay taxes. Earning $100 million of revenue in a year?! There are small nations in the world whose gross domestic product isn't that much. One megachurch got robbed on a Sunday and the thief got away with $600,000 in cash from the heist. It was the amount raised during their two services that day, so doing that math, the church might be averaging around $32 million a year in cash donations. That is not counting electronic payments or checks or credit cards, mind you. Thirty-two million dollars, tax-free. If some of these giant churches had to pay taxes, the revenue could reform our public education system, or do some good for the last, the least, and the left-out in our world.

When a place of worship is bringing in that much money, it's hard not to see the supreme hustle behind that. I can understand why people might start a congregation. If I was a less honest person, one who wasn't petrified of eternal damnation, I might do the same. We would have Mary Mary come and sing "Blame It On the Jesus" at the opening, and then Bebe and Cece Winans will be guests on Harvest Sunday, because their love songs for Jesus are everything everyone needs. And the church would be called Holy Rock of Ages Hold My Mule Pentecostal COGIC AME Baptist Community Church. Our ushers would wear the finest in red crushed-velvet robes, with matching gloves. But since I'm trying to stay on Saint Peter's VIP list, I cannot even.

Don't get me wrong. Megachurches in and of themselves are not bad. Maybe you've been blessed to lead thousands of people because you happen to be anointed. But some of these giant churches are built in neighborhoods where most people are living in abject poverty. There are far too few that work toward building up the condition of the very congregation they purport to serve, and far too many wealthy shepherds with starving sheep. That cannot be holy. The road to hell will be littered with the gator shoes of crooked pastors and other "holy" men. They'll get to heaven's gates one day, trying to hit Saint Peter with the "I'm outside, open the door" text, and Saint Peter will be all "New phone. Who dis?"

Religion got more problems than that Team Bad Decisions cousin we all have and remain Facebook friends with because they keep us humble. People are being told to pray their illnesses away, as if medicine (or therapy) couldn't be Jesus's tool to help you get better. People are being told to repress anything sexual about themselves if they aren't married. There are threats of fire and brimstone if you make small mistakes, and they cause people deep psychological scars. Organized religion, practiced fundamentally and literally, is a strong tool of control. So I understand why people do not believe in it or a higher power.

I do not judge atheists for being nonbelievers, because to place trust in some unseeable, untouchable being who is nowhere and everywhere is an intensely personal thing to do. Especially in a world where there is so much suffering. Many of us who have faith struggle with a God who allows so much evil and so many bad things to happen. It makes sense for people to think there isn't a God. The lack of tangible, reproducible proof of the existence of a God or higher power makes it completely understandable. It is your prerogative to think there is no God or ghosts or angels or heaven.

However, some atheists carry a badge of killjoy. Have you ever mentioned God or some higher power in front of an atheist friend and had them basically laugh in your face? Sir. Ma'am. I know you're Captain Cynicism, but just because you can't find joy in the idea of God doesn't mean you should be a perpetual Debbie Downer. You say, "God is good! I woke up this morning," and they retort with, "Or maybe your heart just kept pumping blood. But okay."

Can I live? Can I have my good feels? Did you have to be the wet, dank blanket on my life? Fine, I'll go tell someone else my testimony. When you are made to feel like you're an irrational nincompoop for having faith, you realize that extremism one way or another—whether it's blind faith or staunch skepticism—is counterproductive.

I am not knocking anyone for not believing in anything, but I have to say that it's hard for me to think that the entirety of this world—the plants and animals and just *being*—is random.

Atheist, Christian, Muslim, seeking, or not, I do have a firm belief that we are all connected.

When I look up to the stars at night and see them twinkle, I wonder if they were designed by a Master Architect who just wanted to give us something pretty to look at, even through the ugliness of life. When I see a diagram of the atoms that make up our bodies, and they look identical to those very stars, I cannot help but think it connects to how we're all made from the same dust the universe is. When I see a scan of the brain and it resembles a map of the Milky Way, I am moved to believe that it's because everything that exists is also a part of us. Then I want to sing "Kumbaya" and hold hands with everyone . . . but I'm not sure if they washed their hands. And even though space dust might be in them, so are bacteria. Never mind. Let's connect from afar.

For me, life is easier with the thought that there is some order in all this chaos. I cannot cope with the disasters, tragedies, and heartbreaks that happen every day thinking that it is all some random occurrence with no lesson or purpose or connection to something greater. I cannot get out of bed in the morning not thinking our existence is being dealt with by a force we cannot see. Thinking that there is nothing beyond our flawed, selfish, accident-prone selves would plunge me into depths of despair. My faith is my comfort, and my spirituality connects me with the grand scheme of things. I am but one pin in the cushion of life, but because I am part of everything, I am bigger than I could ever imagine.

I don't believe that faith and reason, including belief in scientific theories, are mutually exclusive. There are major scholars who have said that the more they study the world in all its intricacies, the less they can explain things, and the more they believe in a higher power. This is because science cannot explain many things, try as it may. Science and spirituality do not have to be completely different systems. For example, if the goal of science is to study patterns in systems, and spirituality is a belief in a master architect, couldn't it be possible that the creator designed patterns in nature for you and I to understand creation better? Didn't the three wise men look to the stars for guidance to help them find sweet, newborn, caramel-complected, alabaster six-pound-ten-ounce baby Jesus? That was totally prehistoric Google Maps.

When I am asked why I'm a Christian, I cannot give an answer that will convince anyone else to become one. I am not an evangelist. For me, faith is a lifeline. I think about my life, and I see something has ordered my steps: Someone has made sure I met the right people. Someone has allowed me to prosper in spite of myself. It must be so, because there are too many things I cannot explain. Because in my heart, I know I am a child of God. Because when I am brought to tears about my life, I need someone to glorify. Because I believe that I am a product of God's grace and I hold that love doctrine to heart. Because when I hear music, I feel like it was divinely created. Because when I say a prayer I feel myself at ease in the world. I am a Christian because the idea of someone sacrificing their life for mine makes me swell with pride, and it lets me know that I am worthy. Sometimes I also think really delicious chicken is God's way of saying He hasn't given up on us yet. GLORY, HALLELUJAH.

Also, I believe our very existence is proof that there's something/someone/some things greater than all of us, and different from science, at play. We are walking miracles, and to think it just came together from some Big Bang doesn't curl all the way over for me. Our very existence is against every single odd. For me, a higher power (God) seems to be behind it. There is just too much that we cannot explain.

I honor that power through my Christianity. I believe in the Jewish carpenter who served the poor, saw the humanity in a prostitute, and sacrificed his life so our flawed selves could live. And sometimes, when He was tired of our shenanigans, even flipped a table or two. I am a Christian because I've seen more than I could explain, and it keeps my side-eye for religion as a whole at bay. When I was five years old, in my house coloring on a Sunday morning, someone walked in looking dejected and grief-stricken. Before they spoke up, I was like, "Grandpa died." I had just seen him a few hours before when he was on his way to church, and there was nothing on earth that should have let me know that. But I knew. Some people call it energy, some people call it God. For me, I feel I've been tapped into the divine since an early age, and it is my choice to carry it with me for the rest of my life.

I do not expect or even try to convince anyone else to be religious or practice any spirituality. Your faith, your choice. Just walk in love and try not to be a hateful shrew and you'd be doing life right. The Bible can be a guide, but you don't need to be able to quote Scripture to be a good Christian. How you live is what really speaks for your faith, more than the words you say. None of what Grandma taught me (and none of what I know is true) said, "Use Jesus as your crutch and savior when you do or say something stupid." People are so great at being hateful douche-canoes and saying they're doing so on behalf of Christ. Religion is supposed to be a user's guide to good living, but good people don't need a Good Book to know they shouldn't be intergalactic imbeciles. And terrible people just like to use it as justification for their awful ways.

And yet with all the glory and wonder that God and a faith community can bring, we stay invoking the name of the Lord for our couthless behavior, and that ain't right. Matthew, Mark, Luke, and John didn't evangelize just for us to be out here using God as a Get Out of Jail Free card. I know Jesus paid for our sins, but they didn't break Wonderbread at the Last Supper so we can be lying on Him like this. The part that slays me slowly is when people do a terrible thing and then they say, "Only God can judge me." NAH! I can too. Folks are good for hitting you with the "He who has no sins, let him/her cast the first stone" line. NOPE. I'm throwing a proverbial rock at your head, because your messiness should be called out. Every entity needs checks and balances, and people are outchea running amok in the name of the Father, the Son, and the Holy Ghost. I'm Christian, and my side-eye to many religious institutions doesn't make me any less faithful. All shepherds shouldn't be followed blindly by their sheep. A sinner is just a saint who fell down, right? Well, some of us sinners fall down, stay there, and then use God as the reason why we wallow on the floor. No, ma'ams and sirs.

On Judgment Day, I want Christ to start by making a speech about how we didn't know His life and how He totally didn't say all the foolishness we said He did, and how He didn't say gay people are evil because He had bigger fish to fry. Also, the chapter on Adam and Steve was lost on Noah's ark because they didn't get a chance to laminate things before the flood. I want Him to flip the table and whip everyone's ass for libel and slander.

I am judging all of us for allowing religion to essentially ruin us and divide us. Jesus needs to fix it. Buddha needs to bind it. Allah gotta come through and amend it. Vishnu gotta bring some Velcro to get us back together, and Zeus can zip it up. I'll send a telegram to Orisha to overhaul it, too. ALL these deities need to come together and tell us to get our lives right, because humankind needs its edges snatched for what we do in the name of religion. We do not know how to behave.

Alls I know is that you can't represent hate, misogyny, discrimination, and lack of common sense while saying you're acting on behalf of Christ or any other celestial being. Get some decorum about your lifespace. Saints and Aints, let us live life well and good, but please leave Brown Baby Jesus out of your shenanigans. AMEN? Amen.

Social Media

I was an early adopter of a lot of social networks. I've been on Facebook since July 2004, five months after it first launched. I've been on Twitter since September 2008, back when it still prompted you to tweet with "What are you doing?" I was on AOL Instant Messenger in the nineties, when dial-up was all we had, and if someone called your house you'd get logged off and be mad as hell. You had to deal with that running-ass yellow dude who struggle-pinged his way into Internet connection, often only after twenty minutes and five tries. Social media has been a part of my life for at least half of my life; I am of the bridge generation that remembers life before it was prominent but grew up with it and now cannot imagine life without it.

Social media has come to define my generation and those younger than me, and it has shaped everything about what we do and how we do it. This has been a gift and a curse, because we've lost some interpersonal communication skills as we've gained tech savvy. It's interesting how we correspond now more than ever because of platforms like Twitter, Facebook, and Instagram, yet we are failing at basic communication worse than ever.

Your social-media experience is completely dependent on the people you've curated and let into your space. The people you friend, follow, and like determine what your eLife looks like; I don't know about you, but MY Facebook experience is mostly a good-ass time with many brilliant people who make me guffaw everyday. But then some people you friend and follow will make you roll your eyes so hard that you go temporarily cross-eyed. I am judging these social-media antimavens.

#Hashtag #I #Hate #Your #Hashtag #Abuse

 Hashtags: Sometimes I rue the day they were invented by Al Gore. I really, really do. In case this is 2050 and you're just picking up this book because it is a modern classic, please know that there was a time before we put the pound sign (#) in front of everything. There were some good old days before we thought everything we wrote needed to be a phrase that is squished together with # in front of it. This chapter is dedicated to the memory of those days of yore.

Being the social-media historian (I saw that title on LinkedIn) that I am, let's talk about how hashtags started and what they were originally for. Word on these eStreets is that in the late 1990s (aka medieval times), they were used in some chat rooms. But in August 2007, a man named Chris Messina (a regular dude, not the actor) tweeted about people using # to group stuff. That was all she wrote, and the hashtag became a thing, and Twitter started aggregating hashtagged posts in 2009. Facebook was tardy to the party, only recognizing them in 2013.

Placing a pound sign before a word hyperlinks it and allows it to become trackable, so everyone using that word or search term can find out what everyone else is talking about. In this way, it is really useful. Movements have been started from hashtags on Twitter (*see*: #BlackLivesMatter). People have been dragged by their eyebrows to complete hilarity from some of them (*see*: #PaulasBestDishes). And we're able to have remote water-cooler conversations about our favorite TV shows because of them (*see*: #GoldenGirls).

Hashtags then evolved into random asides, "under the breath" statements or whispered afterthoughts. Example: "Did you see that awful article? #FixItJesus." It's cute when used correctly. People throw all types of shade in hashtag form, and it can be brilliant. Brilliant, I say!

But it's too bad people ruin everything. This is why I must judge us for our hashtag abuse. Yes, you. I know you've done it. And you're probably like, "Luvvie, I don't curr! I love my hashtags and I will use them!"

To which I say: "I know you do, punkin, but you make me wanna pop out the number 3 on your keyboard so you can never make a pound sign again." *Smizes* I blame the day hashtags were activated on Facebook and your cousin who didn't really understand them started abusing them terribly.

What does using a hashtag badly look like? I'm glad you didn't ask.

1. Hashtagging every word of a sentence

I have seen one too many people type a whole sentence, placing a pound sign before every word. #Are #you #seriously #doing #this? I get irrationally irate at this. Why are you placing a pound sign before every word?! Why do you want me to come to your house and find your keyboard and slam it against the wall? I just want to Hulk out at this. It makes reading a chore. I do not want every word I'm reading to be highlighted. Plus, the pound sign breaks up the words and breaks up flow. Also, it is pointless. It's not a random aside, and the words being hashtagged aren't even words that anyone would search. That brings me to the next hashtagging sin.

2. Hashtagging basic words

There are people in the topsy-turvy world who hashtag words like #the, #of, #this, #to, and #for. Why? Because they really enjoy using pound signs and they think their words get lonely without a pound sign to keep them company. Why, in the name of all that is good, are you turning prepositions and sentence articles into hashtags? Seriously. STAHP. You're better than this. I believe in you, and you must stop this. Also, if you go back to the original point of a hashtag, which is to segment conversation and allow people to search a particular word to see what folks are saying about it, you'll know why it's really goofy to put a pound sign on prepositions. Who is searching for the word "the"? NO ONE.

3. Hashtagging a complete sentence

Why do people hashtag complete sentences? #IWonderWhy TheyDoItBecauseItsCompletelyUnnecessary, and they are clearly hell-bent on making my blood pressure go sky high. First of all, that is no longer a random aside. Second of all, doing this makes your words so much harder to read, and what I wrote above isn't even as bad as it gets. I capitalized the first letter of each word, but people who hashtag whole sentences often do not. So you're playing Riddle That Line to decipher what they're trying to say. You, hashtagger, have taken the random aside too far. That's just a sentence you should have written out normally.

4. Using thirty-five hashtags in one post

You just posted a picture and then decided to use eleventy hashtags in the caption. I want Instagram, Facebook, Twitter, Vine, and LinkedIn to have a special forum about you where they suspend your ability to use hashtags and the only way it can be reinstated is if you promise to get your eLife together and never do that again. We have all seen that person who posts a picture of the sky on Instagram with the caption: #sky #blue #clouds #day #peace #love #hope #yup #picture #followme #ITookThis #ForReal #beautiful #lovely #DontDoThis #IBegOf-You #YouAreBetterThanThis #STOPITNOW.

I hope those people go to the market and their favorite fruit is the only thing NOT on sale. I know why people use so many hashtags in their pictures: some terrible social-media strategist has told them that hashtags make their pictures easier to find. But who on Yahweh's earth is searching for #day to find new people to follow? Please stop with this overuse. It makes you look desperate for followers. I know we all are, and whoever says they're not is lying like good baby hair. But try to at least hide it better by not vomiting hashtags over everything.

5. Hijacking an unrelated hashtag

Since hashtags are searchable, and people use them to find what is relevant to their interests, douchebags will use a hashtag that has nothing to do with their post. This is so their content can piggyback on the hashtag's visibility. What they don't understand is that when people see their post has nothing to do with what they're looking for, they will keep it moving and ignore them. You placing the hashtag #Beyoncé on a cup of milk might make people see your picture, but they will probably report you as spam because clearly you're a troll and you cannot be in their eSpace.

Yes, you can take a picture of your Starbucks cup. No, you probably shouldn't tag it with #NaturalHair, thirst bucket. People are notorious for hijacking the hashtags of nonprofits and causes just so they can be in the stream. Why are you so parched to be seen that you're tricking people into seeing your post? That's sad, and you should probably see someone about that.

6. Creating a word that makes the hashtag not work

It's easy to tell who doesn't really understand hashtags, jumping on the bandwagon because they thought it looked cool when their niece or nephew used it in a status. Your aunties and uncles love using a pound sign at the end of a word or phrase, and I just want to send them a message telling them they don't even go to this school. Exhibit A: ThankingGodForLife#. That ain't how that's supposed to go. This isn't "Bring a Pound Sign to Work Day." The tag needs to be in the FRONT.

Some people will use a hashtag before *and* after their word. #Blessed#. NOPE. Take it back. Take it back right now!

Some folks love hashtagging any old thing, even words with apostrophes, not understanding this will make them unsearchable. #I'mSoFavored." You probably are. But you're also doing this wrong. Go get your teenager to teach you, because you're embarrassing them.

7. Being unable to NOT hashtag

The hashtag has permeated everything we do now, to the point that some people have found themselves officially without the ability to NOT place a pound sign in front of their statuses. You cannot recall the last time they wrote something that wasn't hashtagged to death. You think they signed a contract with Hashtag, LLC, barring them from ever posting a status that isn't hyperlinked all the way through. In fact, you are thinking about doing an intervention. You want them to give it up for Lent, because surely this has to count as hashtag gluttony. You do not need to use a hashtag on every single post.

8. Hashtagging titles

The popularity of hashtags has spurred a trend that makes me cringe: Newspapers are using hashtags for headlines: #WillHeWinTheRace? Books are being printed with hashtags on the front: #AMemoir. And #ImJudgingThemAll. I already know I'm young-old, but this is one trend that doesn't need to permeate everything, including traditional titles. I hashtagged the chapter before this, though. HA!

Hashtags have become weapons of mass annoyance, and I want us all to do better so we don't look back on our writing and wonder why no one pulled us to the side.

Your Facebook Is My Favorite
Soap Opera

 Henry Thomas Buckle said, "Great minds discuss ideas. Average minds discuss events. Small minds discuss people." Dead white men love getting stuff wrong, man. I love discussing people, and my mind is quite large, judging by my forehead, thankyouverymuch, Henry.

Look: I love guzzling piping hot tea in the form of gossip about people's lives. I thoroughly enjoy minding other people's business, but it's not my fault. It's theirs. People have made it too easy to know everything about their personal business because of social media, especially Facebook. That is the digital Lipton factory, where all gossip tea goes to boil, and I am here for it all the way.

I have never been into soap operas, even when my grandmother (I miss her so much) used to force me to watch *All My Children* with her during my summer breaks. If you're reading this in the far future (or you were born after 1992), we used to have these shows called "soap operas" where everyone was white, hella dramatic, and prone to having long-lost twins, or amnesia, and being really rich. Yes, they were all set in Rhode Island or Nantucket. And each one would go on for thirty years. People used to keep *the same job* for thirty years. I know, crazy.

But who needs soap operas now when we have social-media timelines? Now you can get a similar drama fix by just paying attention to your friends' and family members' Facebook pages. It's *Days of Our Lives: Real-Life Edition.*

I especially love that friend (or several) we all have who keeps everyone updated on their dating life, like they're writing Carrie Bradshaw's column. I'll refer to this person as the Bleeding Heart. They make social media interesting, because they're the person who is in love with love, but love might not love them that much. If there were a movie about them, it would be called *Love Is Just Not That Into You.* Taylor Swift would do the entire soundtrack, and Adele might make a cameo on the intro track and slay right quick.

Anyway, Bleeding Hearts wear their hearts on their sleeves and on their statuses. They are the ones who you might have not seen since you were in middle school together, but you can track their entire dating history, including start and end dates, just by going on their page. You can almost chart their cycles in dating, because at this point everyone sees the pattern but them. They're as predictable as the moon but not as bright.

* * *

Stages of the Facebook Relationship: Bliss to Ending

Stage 1: They meet someone and have a date

The Bleeding Heart is single, and they don't like it. How do we know? Because they remind us constantly how much they want love and how happy they'd be if they were in a relationship. It's a pity party and a wishing well at the same time, and you wonder if they meant to send this as an e-mail to their best friend instead of making it a public Facebook status. Sometimes, it's an audition, too, because they will post thirst-trap pictures, and we all hope someone falls into the trap they've set. We want them to find someone so they can stop begging the universe like they're in a nineties R&B video. They probably spend many a night staring out a window as it rains while rocking silk pajamas.

This is when the Bleeding Heart lets us all know that they're going on a date. They're not going to make the status just that plain, though. They inform us about their impending outing by having us help them pick out an outfit. Or they ask a question like, "Where should I take someone that will be cheap and creative?" And everyone is genuinely excited to help crowdsource this fun event. Well, everyone who hasn't been their Facebook friend for a while and so doesn't already know that this is something that occurs so often that it's lost its luster.

Anywho, they settle on that fancy date to Olive Garden because a Never Ending Pasta Bowl is a great way to get to know a potential bae better. They get dressed in their finest Friday night duds that look good but don't look like they tried too hard. They take that full-length-in-the-mirror-before-stepping-out selfie and upload it so everyone can tell them how hot/adorable/cute they look, with the caption "Date tonight! #Cute #Boots #Sweater #Kisses #Follow4Follow #FridayNight #TGIF #SlayingALittle #Black #Blue #Denim #MightDrink #BreadSticksAreHappening." So then I'm forced to start praying that they get basil from their pasta in their teeth because *why all these damb hashtags?* Okay, you know where I stand on this.

The date happens, and they make sure to post a picture of their food and their date's, but never show enough of the other person that we can identify who they're going out with. You know, because they like their privacy (*coughs*). After the date, they post a status saying things went well and they really clicked and it was a beautiful time. And so it begins.

Stage 2: The dating commences

Soon, that one date becomes several, and they start posting statuses about crushing and being smitten. They're being all coy, and cute, and as unsubtle as a toddler's coloring habits. They post emojis of a blushing face randomly, too, just so people can know they flush scarlet at the thought of their new companion. Then, when people ask them for details, they all of a sudden want to be discreet. Everyone resorts to seventh-grade tactics, with "OOOOHHH YOU LIKE SOMEONE," and sometimes their BFF will throw in an inside joke to which the Bleeding Heart replies with giggles. Sometimes, this stage makes you (read: me) wanna gag yourself with a spoon. You are a fully grown thirty-five, and three dates has turned you into a middle schooler? Bless your heart.

Stage 2 is also when they must post pictures of the flowers and Edible Arrangements that their date sent to their job, because you know it's not real until you get that surprise delivery. Get it, boo-to-be! There's always that person in the peanut gallery there to assure them that "he's a keeper."

Stage 2.5: Love quotes

They start posting nightly quotes about love and how it makes your heart lighter in your chest and the sun rise earlier every day or some corny shit that Nicholas Sparks would be proud of. They scour Pinterest for love buttons and post them all over their Instagram as they digitally swoon all over the place. Love is brewing for sure in their land, and they just can't help it. The kiss-face emoji is often abused here, but you're happy for them that things are going well.

Stage 3: Facebook official

Next thing we know, after three serious dates and so much eBlushing that you want to ask them if they have a fever in real life, the Bleeding Heart takes that giant step: they change their Facebook relationship status to "In a Relationship with Bae S. Bae." They are so excited to let the world know, and this status change comes with a soliloquy on how they have found their backbone in Bae. Their BFF is all, "FINALLY. I was wondering when you'd put it up," and puts up a smug emoji so everyone can know they knew first and were in on it. Ain't nobody care, though.

Other people rain down congratulations on the newly taken eFriend as if they just won a blue ribbon at a dating derby. I want to comment, "Yay, congrats on finally having asked them, 'Where's this going?' So brave!" Or, basically: "Glad your lonely ass finally found someone so you can stop telling us how lonely you are." It's like a verbal slow clap full of shade.

Shout-out to you for finding someone who thought you were worthy of giving their last piece of chicken. That really is how you know it's love. Personally, we need to be married with three kids before I bestow that honor on you. The only person who's earned it so far is my mom, and that's because I figure when I take up space in your womb for nine months, I should probably not be stingy about my yard bird with you.

The hands we've all been seeing in the carefully composed pics that revealed nothing about who they're dating finally come with a face and a name (and a link to their Facebook profile). So we all click through to see more about Boo-thang. Aaawwww, they're FAHN/cute/okay-looking/will have to do I guess.

Now, with this "In a Relationship" thing established, they must tell us about everything their boo said in that conversation that made them laugh so much because he/she/they is the funniest person ever. And aren't they so great and witty? And everyone hits a pity "like" just so the Bleeding Heart gets some sort of response and their status isn't left in some awkward silence.

Stage 3.5: Couple albums

Secure in their relationship (status), the Bleeding Heart now starts creating entire Facebook albums dedicated to Bae. We see the visual evolution of their relationship in the form of so many sappy pictorials. We see clearer pics of that first date (because you recognize the alphet you helped them pick). There they are on the Ferris wheel with their head on Bae's shoulder. But you wonder who the hell took the photo, because all hands are visible in the picture. Do they go on dates with a photographer? How do you have so many intimate pictures in these weird spaces together and neither of you took them? Or are they asking strangers? Surely they must have asked the waitress to take the picture of them both drinking from the same giant margarita glass.

They basically create a virtual exhibition titled "Us: The Relationship," and everyone is invited to their constantly updated art show. At this point, I'm usually emotionally invested in the characters in this telenovela, and I'm rooting for them. I know this is only the first installment in the series, but I'm hoping this is the one where they finally get their Happily Ever After because they have touted this person as the "love of my life."

Stage 4: Trouble in paradise

Eventually, the lovey-dovey statuses start popping up less frequently as the luster of new love starts to wear off and the honeymoon phase ends. All of a sudden, the Bleeding Heart starts posting passive-aggressive statuses about loving and not being loved in return, or about people who don't deserve to be trusted. There might be some vague shots about people who make you fall without planning on catching you. There might be something about exes who don't know their place. Those of us who are watching this movie start picking up what they're dropping. All is not well in Bae-land.

If the shit is legit about to hit the fan, Bae responds to one of their shady statuses with something snarky. This is when I scoot my chair closer to the computer and start making calls. "Girl, did you just see that? Are they fighting? I think they are!" And me and my BFF start getting our Sherlock Homegirl on, putting two and two together to figure out when things started going awry. We can plot the precise point where things took a turn for the worse. It is sometime between their last "I LOVE YOU, BOO OF LIFE" status and this miffed state they're in. We go back through the photos for visual evidence, too. If only I used my powers of investigation and deductive reasoning for good, instead of in petty situations that have nothing to do with me.

Even though I'm keeping my wits sharp by conducting such in-depth analysis of the state of their relationship, I am wondering why the Bleeding Heart is choosing to handle their conflict on this main stage. Why do they need to post this stuff to a thousand of their non-closest acquaintances?

Stage 5: The breakup

Well, things start getting bad when the Bleeding Heart removes Bae's name from their relationship status so it just says "In a Relationship" and the "with Bae S. Bae" part is gone. Then, it becomes "It's Complicated." What that means is "I'm basically single, but I don't want to announce that yet because I'm hoping we can work things out. Things are just really hard right now, and I don't know where we stand, but I'm pretty sure we're done." It's really only complicated to them, though, because odds are Bae has already called an ex. Basically, you're in a relationship by yourself at this point. I call it a "love monologue" because y'all don't go together anymore but only one of you realizes it. Sad. It's also important to point out that no one over the age of "good and grown"—i.e., twenty-one—should ever consider "It's Complicated" as a relationship status for Facebook. Scratch that. I'll make it twenty-five, because I'm feeling generous.

This is when me and my BFF congratulate ourselves on such a thorough investigation. We're the relationship version of Miss Cleo. Oh, gosh, you don't know who that is, do you? She was this fake Jamaican psychic who used to do infomercials. Ugh, never mind. You're too young/too far in the future to remember. Google her, though. And cackle.

Stage 5.5: Facebook officially done

The five albums of couples pictures posted between February and July disappear in a flourish one day. Then, finally, the Bleeding Heart changes their relationship status to "Single," and Facebook informs everyone of this fact with a broken heart in their news feeds. This usually happens after they've dealt with the acute hit to the ego. You can almost hear the sad trombone, because this was the relationship they were hoping would lead to a trip to Jared's. People immediately comment with their condolences and sorrys. "OMG, are you okay?!" Their name might as well be Annie, and they've been struck by a smooth criminal. Of course they aren't okay!

There are always the people who are tone-deaf enough to ask "What happened?" How is that appropriate? If you don't know what happened, odds are you don't need to know. Some will even offer up their ears for support. "I'm sorry to hear this. Let me know if you need someone to vent to." Ma'ams and sirs, if you're finding out someone's relationship ended from a Facebook status change, you're probably not the friend they want to cry to in this time of need. Play your position, acquaintance. You're supposed to be on the bench, and you think you're the starting point guard.

Some friends will comment about how they just knew that boo was not right for the Bleeding Heart. Comments like "Don't worry! You were too good for that joker anyway!" will fly. Those friends usually end their attempt at comforting words with some cliché quote about other fish in the sea and how love is all around them. Thanks for nothing, NOPRAH! What if they get back together? What then? Do you take back what you said? Maybe what you need to do is drink a cold glass of HUSH. You shoulda just lurked like the rest of us did. Who asked you?

Then the best friend pops in to reassure us that all will be well, and like they told their bestie in that two-hour conversation post-breakup, this was all part of a bigger plan and with everything comes a lesson. Because you know BFF must let everyone know they knew about the breakup before it became official on Facebook.

If we're lucky, the Bleeding Heart will proceed to go through the heartbreak publicly, and they will spill the tea on what happened. If they're especially petty, they will tag ex-Boo in an angry Facebook status, telling us why their ex ain't shit, and I will wonder if they've forgotten that the person who is now terrible was just their partner. Doesn't that call into question your ability to make sound judgments? Bless it.

In spite of all this drama, sometimes the Bleeding Heart makes up with Bae and goes back to Stage 2. We side-eye them from afar because that didn't last long, and all their theatrics were for what? Now we know they're just "that couple" who will do the on-and-off thing. They're like a relationship yo-yo: up and down.

Other times they are truly done with that boo, and they eventually restart Stage 1 with a new person. You're there to eat it all up because you already know they will keep you updated. You order a new tin of cheese-and-caramel popcorn (shout-out to the Chicago mix!) and you get ready for another round of "Why Don't You Love Me?" Bless their achy breaky hearts for perpetually publicly failing in their private lives. As if getting your heart dropkicked through the goalposts of life isn't bad enough by itself. Doing it with an audience has to be extra shitty—but you're the one who created this movie and bought everyone a ticket.

And then I'm left wondering what they're gonna do with that neck tattoo they got of Bae's name. Will they cover it up with a rose or the face of a cat? I will stay tuned, because they'll be sure to post a selfie from the tattoo shop.

One day, the Bleeding Heart might get married, and since we've already seen them go through the Facebook relationship cycle so often, we are all genuinely happy that they made it to the Love Promised Land. On the way to that destination, they updated their statuses more often than Facebook pushes out their mobile app updates. It's been a long road, but here they are. They will create an official Facebook event for their wedding, with details about the reception. They'll even make sure they message their favorite Facebook friends asking if they got the invitation and if they will be attending. Because why not turn your special day into an occasion for you to meet people you've been eFriends with for a while but whose phone number you don't have? I mean, these eFriends have been with the Bleeding Heart through five very public relationships and breakups, so why not pay $150 a plate to feed these strangers at the reception they insisted on making too big even though they know good and damb well they cannot afford it. They will change their Facebook status to "Married" the moment after they say "I DO," and you want to offer them some Sprite since they obeyed their thirst so properly. They couldn't even wait and enjoy their ENTIRE wedding day to make that change. But good for them.

I'm also secretly hoping that they had a talk with someone who told them not to share everything about their love life with thousands of strangers. I actually cross my fingers that they stop giving the whole world a twenty-four-hour key to their house full of dirty laundry. When you leave the door to your heart house open, don't be surprised when people come in and eat all your food. Many a Bleeding Heart have changed their relationship status from "Married" to "Single" in a matter of months or a year, and at that point, you just want them to have a gahtdamb seat, because clearly love is being a haterbish to them and maybe they need to do bad all by themselves for a minute or two.

Don't mind me, though. I subscribe to the "real Gs move in silence like gnus" way of life. I like to keep my personal life sacred and away from the eyes and ears of prying people. I have never had my relationship status on Facebook, and I've been on there for more than ten years. I have never uploaded couples albums, and I certainly have never argued with my beloved there. Why? Because that is hallowed ground for me. My relationship isn't for public consumption, and my heart would not know how to heal properly from hurt in a public way.

When I get married, folks will see pictures of my fly-ass gele on the day of as my Nigerian family dances behind me. People will be all, "I didn't even know Luvvie was engaged." Damb right, tricks. The wedding will start three hours later than planned, of course, but attendees will forgive me because I will show up looking like a bag of money, and they'll understand that it taking forever to get me looking like that was worth the wait. All will be forgiven. Will I change my Facebook status? Maybe, maybe not. Who's to say? People will ask why I didn't post pictures of my groom, and I'll tell them to mind their business.

You're probably like, "Luvvie, are you saying we should never talk about our relationships on social media?" No, I am not. I'm just saying that when people are invited onto your love train because you've shared every detail, then you're making it community property. For every broadcasted gesture of love, I hope there are two gestures we don't see because they're yours and yours alone.

But you do what you want and keep sharing every detail of your relationship on Facebook, and I'll keep my floss handy, because popcorn gets in my teeth and I like to stay prepared.

For Shame: Get Some eBehavior

I was loitering on Facebook one night when I got a message from someone I didn't know. He was Nigerian, based on the name, and he rolled into my messages saying, "You are so sexy. Can we have some chat?"

I clicked on his profile, and he had to be about fifty-three at minimum, looking like everyone's slightly greasy uncle. No, sir! We cannot have any chat! I am fresh out of chats, and I checked Amazon and chats are back-ordered until the 32nd of Neverary. Ugh. I bet he sent that message while Aunty was snoring next to him. I reject it and return it to sender, in Father Abraham's name.

Unsolicited messages from random men are an unfortunate rite of passage on social media, and some just make you want to jump in the shower and scrub everything. Nigerian Uncle's message was not the worst I've gotten. At least all he asked for was some chat. Some people will jump straight to vulgar stuff, and then you wonder if they were raised by mannerless wolves.

People lose all semblance of couth and decency on social media, and it makes me want to report them to somebody. Like, where is your mama, and does she know you're being dim online? We are doing ill-advised things online constantly, and I'm judging us for it.

Social-media hookups are not new or novel. It's been a thing since back in the days of AOL when people would be in chat rooms and on Instant Messenger. Countless relationships started with the simple question "A/S/L"—that's "age, sex, location," for anyone who doesn't know because they were too young (or old) to ever partake in those games. Millions of people have met their husbands, wives, concubines, and future restraining-order recipients on social networks. It makes sense for people to troll these platforms for love. You gotta keep your eyes peeled for the next person who will spoon you.

However, you gotta know how to make the magic happen and not be a creep while doing it. There's a thin line between receiving a straightforward indication of someone's intentions and filing a police report on the stranger who makes you feel in danger from behind a computer screen. Ultimately, if your behavior would make your mom frown, think twice. I'm side-eyeing all those people who have turned every social network into their Tinder.

You know what gives me the heebie-jeebies anytime someone does it? Poking me on Facebook. I have been on Facebook since forever, when profiles were one page and you couldn't upload albums. I've watched the site evolve and grow and seen features come and go. One feature that just will not die in the hail of blistering fire it deserves is the poke. They have gotten rid of things like Facebook Gifts, but they choose to keep this poke thing, which is now the spider monkey that will not let go of our eAnkles. It is a boil on all our asses.

The Facebook poke is the never-defined, always-creepy ability to virtually tap on someone's shoulder or poke them in the who-knows-where-you-want-to-imagine. Mark Zuckerberg and his team of evil world dominators refuse to really answer as to what it's for, but that doesn't even matter, because it has taken on its own definition. To poke someone on Facebook is to randomly try to get their attention to flirt. It's a virtual wink, and like winks, the person who sends one your way makes all the difference in the world.

If the poke comes from one of your friends, this might be their way of playfully annoying you. That's cool. But if the poke is from a dude, especially one who is not currently poking you in real life, then it's gross. Fortunately, I have smart friends, so they never poke me. The creeps who do are always dudes I don't know at all, and I cannot deal. I am UNABLE TO CAN[18] with their lack of decorum.

This is not a valid way to express romantic interest. If you're crushing on or interested in someone, and your way of letting them know is through a Facebook poke, you're wack and you have no game. If I wanted to be poked by random strangers, I'd go to a crowded reggae club and walk to the bar, where several bamba-claat will act like they "accidentally" grazed my ass with their fingers. No, thank you! Very few love stories begin with "One day he poked me on Facebook." VERY FEW! And if they did, I want to pull the person to the side and ask how hard he apologized for his error.

That poke is only made creepier when the person who does it has "Married" on their Facebook profile. Have you no shame? This is the gift and curse of our access to people's private information. I will never get over how people who are seemingly in serious monogamous relationships are trolling social media for sex. Folks are creating digital harems for themselves, setting up profiles to be cheating dogs.

The point of some people's entire digital lives is to procure ass. It's like they see every new online connection as potential for a

---

[18]*unable to can*: For when "I can't" doesn't do the job.

new nether connection. I realized this when I started getting people flirting with me on LinkedIn, of all places. That is the most chaste and dry of social networks. Everyone is in their all-white button-downs and blazers, looking like the uptight, hyperserious people they are not. There is little cleavage and no six packs to be seen on LinkedIn, our electronic résumé. This is the platform where instead of lying about our vacations, we're lying about how many words we can type a minute. And we've massaged our positions to sound like they're management-level instead of entry. What part of that place says "Date me"?

No part, that's what.

So how do people still muster up the nerve to try to solicit you there? How? *Is nowhere safe?* Flirting on LinkedIn is like walking into a meeting in the office conference room and asking your coworker to a romantic dinner. If you like them, you better do it after hours and not in that environment.

"Hey. I like you. Let's chat." Look. I like caramel candy, but it gets stuck in my teeth. I'm not sure what liking someone has to do with the price of hot chocolate in Thailand. No, scrub! I don't want your number. No, I don't wanna give you mine. One of my friends had someone send her a dick pic on LinkedIn. She said he was an adult film star, so I told her that maybe he was just sending that as his résumé. Too bad she wasn't hiring. Your romantic LinkedIn message makes me want to spray my computer with Raid, and then it shuts down and I have to restart it. Rude.

Speaking of inappropriate venues, now that selfies are major and we cannot help but turn our cameras to ourselves, folks gotta learn how to behave accordingly. Selfies are not acceptable everywhere. You know what places you should probably not make about your face? A memorial for Holocaust victims, or a former slave plantation, or in front of a burning building, or a funeral. Step away from Maw Maw's casket, fool. Anywhere that is the location of a tragedy or is supposed to honor and remember the dead is a place where you should refrain from taking selfies. Go show your revolutionary self-love or impressive and tone-deaf narcissism elsewhere.

In fact, how people deal with death on social media in general is often insensitive and crass. We are all armed with smartphones, so now we're able to capture footage of everything. Our days are documented and so are our joys and struggles. I scroll through my feeds sometimes, mad as hell that folks are so callous about images of death, treating it like any other thing they just hit "Share" on. I have seen one too many dead bodies or heads blown off without warning on my social media, and it is never anything less than jarring. It is an immediate day-ruiner. People might be sharing a news story, but the featured image is of a lifeless body. First of all, I do not understand how media outlets feel okay making the main image for a story the dead subject's body. That is crude and wholly unnecessary. Then people, of course, pass the story on. I've seen pictures of bodies piled on top of each other after a stampede that killed hundreds. It showed up on my timeline under a picture of one of my friends' newborn babies, and I was just not ready. I've seen auto-play videos of shootings where before you can look away, you've seen someone's blood spilling as they hit the ground.

When called out for their insensitivity, people will often say they want others to feel the pain of the families who have to deal with such loss, with their brothers and sisters being killed. Why should we have to see the lifeless bodies of people before we can come up with empathy? If we need to see blood run from people's skulls to be affected by their deaths, then we are monsters. Even in our outrage, it is a spectacle.

Everyone grieves differently, and we all deal with death on our own terms. However, some are taking to social media to expose people on their deathbeds or in their last resting places. Sharing videos of dying strangers is one (hideous) thing, but some people will go against the conventions of common decency and pass along videos of their loved ones taking their last breaths on Facebook or

Instagram. Misery loves company, but personal trauma should not be such a tangible shared experience.

I've seen folks break tragic personal news to their loved ones on social media. No one deserves to find out that their cousin/sister/son/nephew/grandparent died via a Facebook status. Can people ensure that families have been told before dropping their eulogies? I've seen this happen, and it is always traumatizing to whoever discovers the news this way. It's a double whammy. We're living in the culture of FIRST, but certain things should be treated delicately, even if it's slower.

The only thing that spreads faster than death online is hate and trolls. The Internet is full of people whose lives are so miserable that they want to make sure they play a part in other people's gloom. This is why I am convinced that hell is an eternity spent in the comments section of many websites (especially YouTube and Reddit). People find the strength when seated behind a computer to spew the most vile, disgusting things they can think of. Keyboard courage is indeed real, and the hateful dirt bucket behind the computer screen is often some lonely person living in their mama's basement, scratching their ass, and lacking vitamin D because they refuse to go outside.

From the thumb thuggery to the creeps to the inappropriate selfie-lovers, everyone needs to have a gahtdamb seat from time to time and check their behavior. If it'll make their mom frown and if it shames their family name, they should think twice.

Dumbed-Down News

I was on Twitter the night of January 12, 2010, when a massive earthquake hit Port-au-Prince, Haiti. Hours before news of it broke on television, I was reading about it via the Twitter account of a man named Richard, who ran a hotel that was in the middle of the city, but was still standing amidst the rubble. There was no electricity and according to him, they were using flashlights, candles, and anything else they could find to see. I kept on refreshing Richard's timeline, thirsty for updates, because as I listened to the news, nothing I was hearing was as compelling as his tweets. He was *in* the disturbance, and he informed us at the moments there were aftershocks. People were tweeting at him to see if he somehow had news of their loved ones, and he responded as well as he could. My friend's husband happened to be in Port-au-Prince doing some reporting, and when this news hit, she was incredibly worried because she didn't know his whereabouts. But he was staying at the hotel that Richard managed! So she sent a tweet to him and asked if he had met a man named James (not his real name). She described her hubby and waited.

She got a response from Richard the next morning, a couple of hours after sending the tweet. He told her that he had been with her husband earlier and he had gone back out to do what journalists do, report. It was the first time I cried over a tweet. I was so happy for her! It was like that good news was for me. If any moment could capture the power of social media to send us information and news right when we need it, that was it.

Someone unknowingly live-tweeted the assassination of Osama bin Laden when he posted a tweet saying he heard helicopters in the quiet town of Abbottabad, Pakistan. I've been on Twitter when numerous major events have happened, and each time, I am awed by how technology and the World Wide Web have made our possibilities for connection limitless. They expand our worlds, and they connect us to people all over the globe. I was there as a rescuer tweeted about heading out on a speedboat to help the people who were on a plane that crashed into the Hudson River. I remember exactly how I felt the moment I saw the tweet saying that Michael Jackson had died, and how comforting it was to share my grief with countless people who felt the gut punch just as hard as I did.

Social media has transformed our ways of communicating, and it has turned journalism on its head. I praise this aspect of the changed media landscape because at its most beautiful and useful, we get moments like my friend connecting with Richard in Haiti. The digital age has also allowed the rise of citizen journalists; people can tell stories that combat the false narratives spread by the mainstream media. You can live-tweet what is actually happening at a protest, so there's a different perspective from the tales of violence and mayhem on the nine o'clock news. You can write a blog post about the state of education in your district, so that when funding is cut, we have the stories of those who are actually affected. You can bring people along with you as you experience things firsthand. That is the awesome power of social media.

However, it's not all progress and nuance in the news. I am judging us for the way digital platforms have mutated how we report and engage with news and led to the dumbing down of our ideas and our critical thinking.

Everything about the news has shifted, from the way we consume it and report it to even the things that we deem worthy of reporting on. Social media and digital technology have changed the very business model of journalism. Where newspapers and magazines used to reign supreme, now they're threatened by our love of instant hot takes from blogs and digital outlets. For the record, I do not think print is going anywhere. Its presence might be reduced, but I cannot imagine it becoming obsolete. As the use of social media to spread and create news rose, though, publications were left scrambling and playing catch up. They should have been the ones at the forefront of the change, yet they were slow to evolve and, as a consequence, they had to follow the trend that was being set without them. But trends come and go. The traditional Big Media (with a big M), which I consider to be television, radio, newspapers, magazines, and their digital presences, should stand straight in the midst of these shifting trends. Instead, they're bending to the pressure.

I want journalism to get back to holding ethics in high regard again. Maybe it's the idealist in me; I like to keep hope alive. I understand that the traditional press is trying to compete by making sure they constantly stay on the pulse of things and report them as they happen. However, this means they are not taking the time to confirm stories, verify sources, and double-check facts. In the culture of "FIRST," it is easy to fall into this trap, because if you aren't first, are you relevant? Yes, yes you are. I think so anyway. You might be behind the ball on breaking the news, but at least people can look to you for the truth.

Playing the game of "FIRST" is not serving us well because as outlets race to tweet and report, they are misreporting important facts, credibility be damned. Too many formerly stalwart publications are rushing and end up getting the stories wrong.

That can't be how it works.

Our media is supposed to be a trustworthy and reliable observer of society, feeding us information on happenings objectively and accurately. However, that is more of an ideal than a reality, and that is why the lack of real journalistic ethics and the speed of dissemination on social media have twisted things so thoroughly. The media is supposed to be the gatekeeper of information, and how they mold it and report it absolutely affects how we consume it and react to it. The increasingly loud failures of traditional press in the era of Facebook, Twitter, and Instagram make me want to just slide off my chair.

Historically, journalists have not been as objective as they could be. Try as they may (and sometimes they do not try at all), their personal biases color their reporting. But these days it's not just biases coloring things, it's the new world of immediate feedback and instant news. The twenty-four-hour news cycle is keeping us in the know, but it is also spreading ignorance through underdeveloped thought and coverage.

Because many breaking news stories now start with a random person sending out a seemingly innocuous tweet, we're turning less and less to traditional sources to get the information we need. The press tries to counteract this by trying to be constantly in the know. When they jump to conclusions that later prove to be wrong, we tell them to do better research. But when they take an hour and a half to confirm that a major celebrity died when that celebrity's friend already tweeted out a confirmation, we also send major side-eye their way. So we're stuck in a cycle of impatience which gets us quick information that is not always quality information. Dambit.

Not only is this demand for instant news gratification careless, it's also dangerous: for example, when a shooting happens and the press tweets pictures of the supposed suspect without confirmation. One too many times, they've been wrong, and the person whose photo is now all over the Internet ends up not being the culprit. Instantly, they've ruined an innocent person's life because they did not do their jobs properly. Reporting publicly on guesses instead of confirmed reports is rookie behavior, but now professionals are doing it constantly. What happens when they realize they were wrong? They make meek and quiet apologies that no one pays attention to. By that point, people have already run with the falsities, because perception is usually more important than the actual truth. As the old saying goes: "A lie gets halfway around the world before the truth has a chance to get its pants on."

I would prefer a later truth than a quicker lie.

Rumors start from whispers in the air and sources that are not reliable, someone's cousin's uncle's sister who had heard from her niece that something happened. When a media outlet that should know better reports something that is not true, we gotta call them to the table to ask where they got it from. You know what kills me softly? The fact that major news outlets who are supposed to be reputable are now not only dropping the ball on doing their own due diligence but placing their trust in smaller, less proven outlets. I saw a major outlet publish an entire article on their website based on a rumor reported by a website that had a "satire" disclaimer at the bottom. Who the hell are we supposed to look to for truth if the people who are supposed to be professionally responsible for providing it are failing so badly? It's one thing for an everyday person who did not go to journalism school or hasn't spent the last seven years in a newsroom to fall for some of these websites. It's another, more hopeless thing when folks who consider themselves to be journalists fall for the okeydoke. If they don't know better, how are the rest of us supposed to? LAWD.

Also, the prevalence of satirical websites makes me want to slice up my cuticles right before I paint my nails. The word "satire," it seems, no longer means lampooning the truth for comedic purposes and making the world look at its absurdity in the mirror. Satire now means "Let me just make up some shit and post it to the Internet." "Satire" and "straight-up lies" are not supposed to be synonymous. This is what happens when your comedy lacks intelligence. It makes me stabby and ragey, and I want to shot-put everyone who isn't *The Onion*. On a list of "Things I Hate Intensely," these busted sites will come in above Spirit Airlines, kale, and yellow Starburst. I wish a thousand crashed servers on each of them. They've made the line between satire and defamation far too thin—you cannot just slap the satire label on anything and go "TA-DA!" I hate it so much.

On the other side of this fake-ass coin, people gotta quit believing everything they see on the Internet. I'd like to quote Martin Luther King, Jr., who said, "Everything on the Internet is not true."

Dr. King was so wise. Just because a statement is in a nifty-looking meme or superimposed on a picture of someone staring at the sunset affectingly does not mean it should be taken as truth. At least once a day I have to tell my Facebook friends that something they posted and are outraged about is fake news. It's my contribution to humanity, since everyone seems kinda slow now. *Everyone*. It crosses lines of class, gender, education, and ethnicity. It is the great equalizer. It's like critical thinking has gone on permanent vacation since social media has dumbed down our ability to receive and analyze information. There are PhDs believing that a site with the URL www.nytimesco.net is actual factual. Pay attention! Jeebus be the fence of discernment around our proverbial sense houses, because we are outchea failing at media literacy.

That celebrity died three years ago, so your RIPs are late and I'm side-eying the hell out of you. No, that white actor is not playing Bob Marley in a new biopic. And no, that Black power couple is not funding a terrorism organization. While I'm here, forwarding that e-mail to twenty people will not mean Bill Gates will PayPal you $30.75. Why must I facepalm so hard? Why do we have to be so gullible in the worst ways? It's all a hot-ass mess.

This little drama plays out across my social-media platforms multiple times a week, where some ridiculous rumor is spreading, aided by someone reputable or "smart" passing it along as fact. The worst part is always how easy it is to debunk. People act like Google went on break and said it'd be back never. It is so frustrating. We have all this information at our fingertips, but we skip over it in favor of reacting quickly, being first, and starting conversation, even around false facts.

Across the board, I have to say that consuming news has become an exercise in "Should I believe this?" now more than ever. We have always been lied to by major media—propaganda is an ever-present part of the press, and this is why we all need to be careful about the messages that are being amplified and how they're being twisted and given new context. We have to stay curious. But now things seem worse than ever. Half the battle is finding out what is happening in the world, and the other half is doing our own research to know what is real, what is half-truth, and what are flat-out lies. I hate that the lies are taking up so much space. When Tammy from Arkansas is posting bullshit on her blog, that is one thing, but when a major media outlet is using the same nonsense to get visitors online, then you know we are stooping to new lows. Who needs accuracy and journalistic integrity when you can have a lot of clicks?

It feels like we're constantly trying to use cheat codes for this news game. I'm sick of this clickbait custom where we're being tricked to take in news by any means necessary. One way people do this is by creating salacious headlines for articles that only exist to pique our curiosity so that we click on them. Reputable publications and blogs alike use misleading headlines to get visitors, and it tap dances on my last nerve. We don't trust ourselves enough to come up with interesting stuff without having to trick people, and we don't trust people to click unless it's trashy, shady, and wanton. Sheesh.

Our headlines have gotten more and more deceptive, and it is leading us astray. Your success as a writer is no longer measured by how good your article is but by how many page views you got.

The perpetual clickbait trap of headlines about folks doing tacky things is disingenuous at best. When people do land on the website to read whatever dirt they think they're getting, they often find a much tamer article than they expected. Trick me once, shame on you. Trick me twice, shame on me. So while sites that do this might get a spike in traffic, they will constantly be in need of new readers, because the next time their work comes across any of my feeds, I will know it's garbage and I will not be entertaining it. We've turned the damb Internet and our news into eCanal Street—counterfeits and knock-offs flooding the market and drowning out real work.

And even the non-disingenuous content is questionable at best. The world is falling apart at its seams, and a news telecast will spend ten minutes talking about the celebrities who had Twitter beef and two minutes on the wildfires ravaging the state of California. YOU ARE SUPPOSED TO BE THE NEWS, NOT A GOSSIP RAG. I cannot even, so I'll just odd.

I know the general public likes levity, and sometimes we need an escape, but can you give us the fluff along with some substance? It's like allowing the child who hates vegetables to eat candy as their main entrée for dinner every week. You are supposed to sit there and tell them to deal with that broccoli before they can have cake. Instead, the media willingly lets us go on garbage news benders. Maybe they shouldn't even try to cover the substantive stuff, because they surely do not know how to act when they do. Watch Fox News as they report on anything race-, sex-, or politics-related and you'll realize that our "gatekeepers" are failing with flying colors. They are like the opposite of "The More You Know."

We really do get stuck in these dreadful cycles, because some talking head will say something repulsive and so offensive that you can taste the bitterness in your own mouth. Social media then explodes with everyone gasping in disbelief because of whatever nonsensical crap was uttered on national (and international) television. Our attention is captivated for days as that person goes on a press tour, doubling down on their dumbassery, reveling in their notoriety as a trending topic. Some of them get book deals, some get reality TV shows, and some increase their lead in the polls about who should become president. Do we sit around and watch people go uncorrected in their bullshit, or do we continue to feed the outrage machine that keeps them in the spotlight? It's hard to figure out what to do, but one thing is sure: people are prospering from being unapologetically offensive, trite, and stupid. And we are tweeting ourselves into high blood pressure and ulcers trying to tell them to do better. All I know is that it is feeding our lowest-common-denominator news loop, and it is officially a beast. Being a pompous nut biscuit is now a publicity strategy, and I don't know what we can do to end the madness.

We have more ways to get our news than ever, which is supposed to be a good thing, because more competition is supposed to challenge you to do better. However, in this social-media age, what it has done has allowed the information business to be a free-rein free-for-all. Old rules of journalistic integrity have been thrown out the window. Everyone has been given the conch, and no one knows what to do with it. Instead of using the new-media landscape to spur us to higher quality, we have instead become sloppier than ever: Tweet first, research later. Post first, rescind later. Guess first, confirm later.

This is why media literacy is important. We need to know when we are being fed bullshit (which is always) by the press, and we need to know where to turn to when that happens (citizens on the ground telling the stories), and then we need to confirm those sources. We must remain critical and questioning because we are being pissed on and believing it's raining. But we can all monitor the trash we're letting in and out and keep ourselves vigilant. Read beyond headlines, call Dr. Google, and don't be a part of the problem. And if the website you got the information from uses Comic Sans as its font, you should not only disbelieve it but vow to never go there again, because they know nothing.

How to Succeed at Business Failure

We are social media–driven not just personally but also in the way our business lives are dependent on it. This is why so many people are failing in their professional lives: they bring bad habits, bad taste, and bad behavior in the way they conduct their business online. I cannot help but judge us for it. We do so many things that deserve epic side-eye, and we wonder why we cannot prosper. What are those things? Let's talk about four of them.

1. You are using Comic Sans font

Just like clothes, fonts speak for you. Some are serious, some are more casual, some are classic. And others are clown suits. The leader of that pack is Comic Sans. Comic Sans is a font that is a joke all the way through. In fact, the person who created it never meant for it to be used for anything besides the software he was testing it for. Somehow, the font ended up in Microsoft Word, and on that day, the world was cursed with a typeface that is not only tacky but persistent. It is the Visa of fonts, except it's everywhere I never want to be. At best, it is appropriate for, well, comics. (Refer yourself to the name.) It is for things we're supposed to laugh at on a very basic level. It can also signal things that are supposed to be for children, like their party invitations. THAT IS IT, PEOPLE. That is all.

Somehow, people think the font is cute and friendly, but what it really is is childish and not appropriate for adult business. Government agencies use Comic Sans sometimes. Sure, our various bureaucracies are an everlasting joke, but they don't have to laugh at us with their font, too. That's just rude. I fear that there is a tombstone somewhere with Comic Sans engraving. How is the person supposed to rest peacefully forever like that? I've seen churches, hospitals, and police departments use this font, and I want to write them sternly worded letters of disappointment. Putting serious messages in Comic Sans is like dropping bad news and then saying "LOL" afterwards. It does not compute, nor does it make sense.

Comic Sans should not be used for anything business-related or anything you want people to take seriously. EVER. NEVER EVER.

As a professional, you should know that I cannot think you're all that gathered if you're using a typeface meant for children. If I see that font in an e-mail, I might think you're joking and refuse to respond. The use of Comic Sans is usually accompanied by text of varying colors, because one bad decision begets another.

I found some old posts I wrote in 2003 and they were in Comic Sans font. That should tell you how terrible they were. Who do we need to petition to make them remove Comic Sans from every piece of software? Can we go to Congress and ask for a policy change? Is there a campaign we can run to ensure the extinction of this awful piece of type? Something must be done. Basically, if Comic Sans was a person, it'd be the dude who wears baseball caps backwards, raises the roof at the party unironically, tells terrible jokes only he laughs at, and describes himself as "really chill" because he tries very hard to be cool—but really he's forty, lives at home with his mom, and doesn't have any plans to do better. He's a great babysitter, and kids love him, but is that the dude you want to represent your business at an important conference? No, because he is immature—nice, but not appropriate. Stop using Comic Sans for business, everyone. Please. For the love of all that is good and professional. Stop. Today. Immediately. Thank you.

2. You still use an AOL or Hotmail account for work purposes

Everyone remembers their first e-mail address. Mine was something wack like vettevette@hotmail.com. I was fourteen; don't judge me too hard. Either way, in the nineties, AOL and Hotmail were the places to be in these new Internet streets. All we were doing was chatting anyway. Then the Internet grew up, and we did too, and we went off to college. Some of us started working. And then Gmail happened, because Google launched their plan to control us all. They did it so right, and we were all able to get rid of our 2Cute2BeStressed@aol.com e-mail accounts. Now we could get firstname.lastname@gmail.com. Some of us kept those old accounts to use as our junk e-mail receptacles. When you sign up for sweepstakes or fantasy football leagues, odds are you do so using those AOL, Yahoo, and Hotmail accounts. That is perfectly fine.

If you are still using AOL or Hotmail as your main e-mail or business e-mail account, though, I am not sure I can do business with you, because you seem like a member of Team Bad Decisions. How can I trust your business acumen when you haven't even upgraded your e-mail life since 2001? How can I know that you'll be on top of things when your online moniker is the equivalent of wearing platforms with goldfish in the soles? You are living in the digital seventies, and we must bring you up to date. Odds are you also use Internet Explorer 6, and your website was built on Geocities, and you think glitter wallpaper is still all the rage.

I got a business e-mail from someone with an AOL account

and it automatically went to spam. I only found it in my spam folder after the person followed up by text when I didn't respond. It was like my inbox was so offended it didn't even want me to see the message. If this were basketball, my e-mail client blocked their shot across the court and then wagged its finger in their face, like, "Nope." Word to Dikembe Mutombo. All I could do was look at this person sideways because I thought they were better than that. To this day I'm not sure I ever did reply to their e-mail. I'm scared that whatever their inbox had is contagious.

Get an e-mail address with an ending that is either gmail.com or your own domain name. Or even get one of those @me.com e-mail addresses. There are so many more professional options that there is no excuse for not letting these old addresses die hard.

3. You annoy everyone with your marketing

Everyone is more accessible than ever now that we're spending multiple hours online every day. This is great for businesses because we can reach people 24/7. However, marketing is not about harassing everyone to be your customer, client, or reader. Good marketing is when you know who would be interested in your product and you find ways to get them to pay attention. It does not mean beating everyone on your friends list over the head with your event, sale, or article. It just does not.

Think of the Internet and your friends, followers, and fans as one big conference room. When you do that, you will understand what behaviors are appropriate and what stuff will make people report you as spam. You should conduct yourself as you would if you walked into a professional event where there are some people you're familiar with in varying degrees and some you do not know at all.

Your friends list is full of people who want to support you, but do not take advantage of them by attaching yourself to their eAnkles and trying to use them as your sole customer base. If you are a club promoter and you're hosting an event, please know which of your friends actually live in your city. Do not send folks in New York an invitation to an event happening in Memphis. It's lazy to "Select All" instead of taking the time to go through your friends list and geotarget your message. Also, I know we've known each other since college, but I'm not coming to any party described as "grown and sexy." Any event where that phrase, "grown and sexy," is on the flyer is guaranteed to be full of immature behavior from people with obligations they refuse to acknowledge. You know good and damb well that when you go to "grown and sexy" night at the club, someone's shoes are gonna get stepped on and it'll turn into an all-out brawl. No, thanks! I'll be at home on my couch binge-watching my favorite nineties shows and eating all the snacks.

Furthermore, do not drop your flyers on people's Facebook walls, either. That's like placing one of your stickers on my car. This is my eProperty, and you will not use it to promote your shenanigans. That's intrusive. Learn some etiquette about you. All this will do is get your post deleted, and you might end up on my persona non grata list. Similarly, do not tag people to your event flyer so it shows up in their photos. And if you have anything in Comic Sans on that flyer, your event has already failed before it's begun. I am not coming, and I will be judging people who do.

I love my fellow writers, and I get that we need people to read our words, but one thing I hate is people posting a piece and tagging fifty-five of their friends to it. This is like going up to fifty-five people, tapping their shoulders, and saying "HEY, READ WHAT I WROTE." That's not cute. First of all, again, our friends *can* support our work, but they are not obligated to. When we do the tagging thing, we're basically pulling them into a crowded room and interrogating them about whether or not they've seen what we did. Don't put folks in that position. If you're in their social-media family, trust that they will see it. And in case you REALLY want that person to read what you wrote, send them a message and say

"Hey, it'd mean a lot if you read this." But do not tag fifty-eleven people to your writing. It's pushy and unprofessional.

There are few things that make me blow smoke out my ears more than the folks who take to Twitter to publicize their work in all types of wrong ways. There are the people who are notorious for tweeting random people with "Follow me back." Never in the history of ever have I been compelled to follow someone who thinks the way they should get more people in their eLives is by demanding it. These are the people who walked into the conference room with their business card in the air, saying "HEY, CALL ME." First of all, are you talking to me? Second, don't yell at me. Third and most important, who the hell are you? You didn't even introduce yourself or nothing. You just rolled up and told a stranger to follow you.

And for the people with mixtapes who send me links on Twitter: I do not work in A&R. I don't work for anybody's record label, and I really don't care about your music. Can you not? How about you don't. My iTunes is still mostly nineties R&B, so unless you're sending me a link to Brandy's discography, I do not want. Don't spam me, bro. I don't know why this is such a thing. Is someone advising people that tweeting a hundred random strangers links to their music is effective promotion? It's like handing a stranger on the street your CD (if you're reading this in the future, they were optical discs with music on them). Why should they have any dambs to give about what you just gave them? Every time a rapper tweets me his mixtape link, an angel loses her ability to do the Running Man correctly. Save the angels. Follow me on Twitter, though! @Luvvie.

4. You call yourself a visionary or something equally pompous

We should all think very highly of ourselves. Confidence will take you far, because thinking you're an awesome person allows you to dream bigger, want more, and expect great things from yourself. However, there is a thin line between healthy self-worth and arrogance (aka Kanye West Syndrome). On our social-media accounts, we have to define our entire selves in these small pockets of digital space. How do you tell people who you are and what you do in these short bios? Well, one way is to use terms that are loaded with symbolism so people can picture what we do.

But you can take it too far by using grandiose adjectives and referring to yourself as all types of monumental nouns. Some of us append these major titles to ourselves, and I scratch my head wondering if they are just using an invisible sarcasm font because surely they cannot be serious. So you're the chief executive president CEO director visionary trailblazer of your company, huh? Yes, here I am, still not knowing what the hell you DO, Tommy. If you're calling yourself a trailblazer, I hope your job is to literally set grass and wildlife on fire to make running paths. Do you work for Runyon Canyon Park? If not, that's pretty presumptuous of you.

Why are you calling yourself a "visionary" on LinkedIn?! What does it *mean*? You say it means you come up with great ideas— well, can you execute them? Because if all you have is a notebook in your house full of genius things you've never done, you should delete your profile entirely. Ascribing that word to yourself really raises the bar too high, and you're coming out of the gate overpromising. People will expect the world and then some from you. Isn't that a lot of pressure to put on yourself? Also, the word is pretty meaningless to use on a résumé or a site that is supposed to be your portfolio. "Lemme search for 'visionary' on LinkedIn," said nobody ever.

If actions speak louder than words, some of us are trying to shout into a megaphone instead of doing the work that will make others shout on our behalf. I read some folks' self-written bios and I wonder if they also invented the Internet and solved world hunger. If you're constantly reminding people of how much of a "boss" or "guru" or "expert" you are, you're probably overcompensating. Those descriptions are supposed to be used *about* you; they are words for other people to bestow on you.

There's a difference between owning your awesome and whatever this inflated-title thing that's happening is. I am not saying that people should be overhumble and downplay their talents. Own your dopeness. However, that dopeness does not need to be spelled out as a tattoo on your forehead or in a fake title on your LinkedIn bio. Let your work speak for you, and someday people might call you the Highborn Leader of All Things in your industry.

All that said, I will call myself an expert at the art of side-eye. I'm also a guru of rice eating. I think I want to add "Grand Wizard of Everything" to my About Me page. I am the CEO, president, grand goon, and executive director of Awesomely Luvvie. Over there, I'm an expert at writing in random slang and the maharishi of wig snatching. You will deal.

Real Gs Move in Silence

The nature of social media is to encourage us to share our lives. This is true. The World Wide Web is a series of wires that connects us all to each other, no matter where we are in the world. And part of the beauty of being together even when we're apart is that we can keep up with everyone's lives. You may not have seen me since high school graduation, but you still know what I'm doing for a living, what my days are like, and who I am sharing them with—well, you'll have an idea, based on what I'm sharing. We get to paint our lives and curate them for those who meet us in our digital spaces, and it is up to us to decide how much of the total experience of our days we pass on for public consumption.

Some of us share everything. Every single thing. We wake up and share a pic of the sun coming up outside our window. We take a shower and we post a mirror selfie. We tweet that we just took an amazing dump. We Snapchat ourselves putting on clothes; the actual process of putting legs in pants is now post-worthy. We are

Generation Overshare, hear us roar and then post a Facebook status about it. I know what you did last summer. And last night. And two minutes ago. I know how you felt through all of it. I know when you're heartbroken (see chapter 15), and I probably found out three minutes after it happened. I know every single thing about your life, because you've kept me updated about all of it.

There are certain types of oversharers online:

1. The Everything Sucks Oversharer

This person might be going through a rough patch in their life. Or maybe you've known them for years and you understand that their life is like the TV show *Good Times*, where they didn't have good times until the show was ending. That show should have been called *Downtrodden and Out*.

Anywho, the Everything Sucks Oversharer is Eeyore. Nothing is ever going well, and you really do start to wonder what life has against them. It sucks, truly, because you wish you could help them. Even on days when nothing of note happens in their lives, they will pour out feelings of worthlessness, and it gets to the point where their posts start to stress you out. You've run out of helpful words for them, and now all you can muster is "You're in my thoughts" and "HUGS." Then you run fresh outta encouraging comments and you just drop an emoticon for support.

This person might be going through a depressive episode. Or just a shitty (entire) year. You know your limits as a Facebook friend or Twitter fan, and you realize that this is cathartic for them, but you also wonder if they have close friends they can go to. Or a therapist, because you're no longer just a listening audience, you're a concerned acquaintance. Is social media their only respite? If so, will they recognize when they've hit a limit where even 2,500 of their closest digital acquaintances cannot help? If ten of your most recent Facebook posts are basically you wall-sliding about life being shitty, your eFriends are probably stressed out on your behalf. They are probably reading your posts and feeling terrible

front of everyone we do not know? Social media and the Internet have allowed us to share the mundane details of our lives with people who don't give a damb. We throw things at the wall, hoping something eventually sticks. We do ordinary things and attempt to get to extraordinary through public validation, likes, and page views. I believe it has lessened our ability to be secure, nonperforming human beings. All the world's a stage, and the Internet is our audience. Generation Overshare has got to stop performing our lives, because we are now actors in our own invisible films. It is not healthy.

Being a part of a larger community of people online is great because we can share struggles, lessons, triumphs, and our lives. However, the phrase "familiarity breeds contempt" comes to mind as we go through our days narrating every single detail, no matter how intimate. The whole Internet has become everyone's journal. Our Facebook statuses sometimes read like the diary you hid under your bed when you were sixteen. "Dear Diary, Today, I lost my virginity." Now it's, "Hey, everyone! I just lost my virginity!" And multiple people comment to tell you congrats. And their friends see that someone lost his/her big V. And so on and so forth.

Sometimes I want us all to go back to being prudes in public and freaks in the dark. You know? Back to the days when only the people closest to you knew your entire business. And back when only the person you were with knew how you wanted him/her to give it to you. I don't need to know that you Nair your face, your love pocket smells like hate, and you're a forty-six-year-old virgin who loves to watch dolphin porn. I feel like everyone needs to go back to just sharing some of this stuff with their diaries, their best friends, their doctors, their cats, and whatever deity they pray to.

Generation Overshare is too anxious to share any and everything happening in our world. People are talking about jobs they *might* get, and people they *might* marry one day, and too many of those mights never come to pass. So many opportunities fall through, so boasting about something that isn't already in your pocket is premature. Just be quiet and wait instead of counting unhatched chickens in public.

Real Gs move in silence like gnats, and I often feel like we need to keep things closer to our chests. It seems like in our perpetual thirst for validation, and with "likes" being currency, we do anything we can to be congratulated for any little old thing.

Maybe I'm just a weird, superstitious Nigerian, but I believe that telling people about something you have brewing jinxes it. Until I sign on a dotted line, I usually keep mum. Some people find joy in your failures. Don't give those folks satisfaction. If you do wanna share your failures, share a lesson too. Not just "OMG, I'm so sad. I didn't get it." Don't mistake your audience for being only well-wishers and friends. Everyone who is connected to you, on your friends list, or as your fan is not necessarily a genuine cheerleader. So pull back a bit. We are opening up our private lives for public consumption, and most of us aren't even getting paid for it.

The Internet cannot replace real life friends who we can call, see (or Skype), and touch. We can start friendships online, but they also need to be accessible if any of our social platforms are shut down. We need to have the phone numbers of those we have learned to love through social media, because if our relationship might end due to a suspended account, how tangible is it?

Real Gs gotta move in silence like gnomes. Tell friends, not Facebook! Use GChat, not Twitter. Go to your therapist, not Instagram.

PART

IV

Fame

We're living in a time where fame seems more accessible than ever before. But one viral video does not make you famous, and neither does having hundreds of thousands of followers on social media. Unfortunately, some of us are reveling in megalomania because of these fleeting things. It's all tinsel: shiny, with nothing substantive behind it.

What do you want to get famous for doing? If the goal is strictly fame without real impact, what's the point?

They say money and fame just makes you more of who you already are. It brings out the youest of yous. Some folks were already smug nuisances. Now just more people know about them.

I am judging us for being fame obsessed. Our pathological narcissism and dehydration for prominence leads us to do some shady and desperate things. All for what? Fame is expensive, and many of us cannot afford it. We should probably not take ourselves so seriously while we're at it. And with visibility comes power and scrutiny and obligations. You can't have fame's perks without its pains.

About Microwave Fame

 The old adage of "All the world's a stage" has never been truer than it is now. Social media has given everyone a voice that they didn't know they wanted or needed and an audience. It's like an ePulpit, where everyone can give a sermon because everyone now has an eMicrophone. "Is this thing on?" Yes. 24/7/365.

Fame has been democratized, and no longer does it mean someone is extraordinarily gifted or talented. Now, it could just mean someone comes up with the right video to post online at the right time. Our fifteen minutes of fame can now be achieved in fifteen seconds with one video that takes off because of foolishness. It could mean you decided to have sex with a celebrity on tape, even though you're technically not a porn star. It could mean you beat your classmate to a pulp while a crowd surrounded you (WORLDSTAR!). Part of what frightens me about being a part of a world where Microwave Fame is a thing and now a goal to add to a vision board is how cheap fame has become.

Actually, that isn't fame: it's infamy. Infamy is rampant and readily accessible, and it is frightening the lengths people will go to rise to levels of notoriety not previously possible. It's positive reinforcement of trifling shit, because what rises to the top is no longer the cream, but the cat hair and dust bunnies that have gotten into the churn. Our Brita filter is hella broken, and I'm not even sure how to fix it.

We're living in a viral culture, and everyone has the fame flu. Folks are so thirsty to be known for anything that I just want to offer them a bottle of Gatorade and a seat. They are parched, and the things people will do to become a big deal on the Internet boggle my mind. The levels folks will go to just for page views leave me floored.

A man created a video to surprise his wife with her own positive pregnancy test. Read that again. Some lady's husband decided to secretly test his wife's urine to see if she was pregnant, and then he created a video about it and uploaded it to the Internet for strangers to see. We have reached peak attention whoredom. You're probably wondering how he pulled it off. Well, his wife usually pees during the night, and she doesn't flush so the sound won't wake up their young child. She mentioned to him that her period was two weeks late, so he decided to sneak into the bathroom after one of her midnight pee sessions. He records himself as he dips a pregnancy test into the toilet. A couple of minutes later, it confirms what he (and she) suspected. The next morning, as she's cooking breakfast for their kids, he walks up and shoves this test in her face, saying, "YOU'RE PREGNANT." She hams it up for the camera in possibly faux surprise, and then addresses the camera, because clearly they have an audience she's ready for. The video went nuts on the interwebs, and then, two days later, they posted another video saying she had a miscarriage. That is when people decided to get science involved, and their research revealed that there is only a tiny chance that pee diluted by so much toilet water can give an accurate pregnancy test result.

Long story long, we all realized that it was a sham. It was all fake.

Those summagoats were lying through their teeth, and I wondered who in the hell left the desperation gates open? How much wrongness can you count in that debacle? The lengths they went to get attention, the intimate thing they were sharing, the fact that in the end, it was all fiction. I am judging us so hard for letting our dehydration for affirmation drive us to foolishness.

People are programmed to want validation and support. Even the most fuck-deficient, don't-give-a-damb person amongst us has someone in their lives whose approval they crave. We all want to be loved and liked. Hell, all living things seem to need validation. One of my favorite quotes is from my favorite book and movie, *The Color Purple*: "Us sing and dance, make faces and give flower bouquets, trying to be loved. You ever notice that trees do everything to get attention we do, except walk?" We all want love, but what ends will we go to get it? The things we are stooping to now to get likes are low-hanging fruit, and it's a shame.

The Internet has normalized a culture of dishonesty. The means (lying and stealing) to justify an end (validation and fame) are becoming cheaper by the day. Not only are people falsifying events in their lives but they're stealing from others to do it. On social media, we create and demonstrate who we are in spurts—status messages, videos here and there, photos. People want to be known as the smartest, the funniest, the richest, and the most interesting. So what are we doing? Instead of actually working to become all of these things, folks would rather take the shortcut of stealing from those who might already be these superlatives. Broke? Why not take a screenshot of the Louis Vuitton luggage set you saw on Instagram and post it as if it were yours? Wanna be known as a leading humorist? Steal people's jokes on Twitter, and pilfer memes and post them like it's your own material. Need to grow the popularity of your Facebook page? Download hilarious videos from YouTube and upload them to your page, giving no credit to the person who created them, and essentially take money out their pockets.

It grinds my gears so damb much. As a creative and a fan of authentic beings, I am disgusted by it. The same way you shouldn't go into a store to steal candy, you should not steal the work of others. However, the Internet's game of Telephone has made it easier than ever to be an idea thief. And I wish I could say cheaters never prosper, but people are being rewarded for their fraudulence. Some folks have built lucrative careers and fame on the Internet by regurgitating other people's content. The message it sends is to do as little original work as possible but be the loudest and you will probably win. It makes me ragey.

Everything is so forged. Some people call themselves "Internet personalities," and I nod my head because it's accurate. They have created personalities for themselves just for the Internet, and who they are offline is completely different. It's fascinating to watch someone on social media and know them in real life and wonder how they're going so far out of their way to be phony. I wonder why they don't feel disingenuous presenting themselves in such a fake way. Aren't you tired of having to be yourself AND somebody else? Isn't that too much work? I am lazy and I can't do it. I can only be one person, because being two requires extra thought, and I'm not a light switch. I can't be "on."

By design, social media is performative. We create the lives we want to live online, curating our days with selective posts about whatever we want to share. We can paint whatever picture we wish by posting the shiny parts of us and leaving the dingy out. My last five pictures might be of me at nice events, but if I haven't posted anything that shows the hefty bags under my eyes, you see all the glamour without the struggle. That lie by omission is common, and even acceptable, because even though it is an airbrushed version of reality, at least it's grounded in reality. We are all lying on some level by not painting complete pictures of our lives, but there are layers to this phenomenon.

When we start lying about our experiences by creating brand new ones out of thin air with Photoshop and Google Images, that is when I will judge us for our pathological need for approval.

A Facebook friend of mine posted a picture of her hotel balcony while she was on vacation, and people commented on how beautiful it was. She reveled in the attention until someone called her out and said that the picture she posted was actually from Google Images. I don't know what prompted them to search for her picture, but they did, and sure enough, it's the default picture that comes up for the resort she said she was vacationing at. Come to find out, some of her past vacation pics were also pulled off the Internet. She was sitting at home, going on fake vacations to impress people who will never set foot in her house. She was Photoshopping herself into pictures in front of monuments, posting them unironically and telling fake stories about what it was like to be in front of Stonehenge. I was at home in my ratty pajamas rolling my eyes so hard that I needed eyedrops to dislodge them from the back of my head. Jesus be a fence and some real-life feel-good for her so she won't feel so reliant on likes. There are a lot more screenwriters out there who aren't even trying to work in Hollywood. They're just using Facebook to create stories, bless their hearts.

We ain't gotta lie to kick it, or to get people to double-tap our pictures. As social media permeates our world, everyone is now in some unofficial competition to live the most interesting life in their online circle. When keeping up with the Joneses becomes a life mantra, you know we are doing too much. We constantly compare ourselves with our friends, followers, and fans. But there is no blue ribbon for "most interesting life," so what are we competing for? We are simply competing for likes, which are arbitrary and have no real-world value. Well, with the exception of people who get paid to be public figures. For those people, likes are currency. When your platform is your paycheck, desperation can reach an all-time high.

The quest for validation is so real that people are buying spam followers for their social media accounts to pad their numbers. Since people are now taking social media to the bank, the higher numbers they have, the more important and popular they seem. We are faking our influence so that people attach more worth to our online standing. In the great Instagram sweep of 2014, some people lost 99 percent of their followers because they were spam accounts they had paid for just to juice their numbers. Instagram cracking down on these accounts and removing them from the platform had people shutting down their accounts in embarrassment, because they were exposed as having spent money on the least tangible of returns. I've seen Facebook fan pages with 400,000 fans, but every picture posted there only gets three likes. The polygraph says YOU ARE LYING. Fake followers do not comment or interact with you. It's like someone paying for some clouds when they need something to sit on.

So who are we doing it for? From the oversharing life to the share-anything-you-think-will-get-likes culture, we're living as our most inauthentic selves. We're losing ourselves in the shells we've created for public display and we are living lies for likes. We're telling people we have jobs we don't, relationships we've imagined, and personalities that are purely aspirational. We are being owned by spaces we're supposed to be owning, allowing them to mold us instead of the opposite. We are social media's Play-Doh, and some of us are too impressionable to remain who we originally were. We are doing anything to be validated, when the only thing we need to be doing is living life loudly as ourselves. Maybe if we did that, we could sleep at night without resting in the bed of adoration from strangers around the world.

We are stuck in a validation vortex, and we're dizzy with desperation.

So You're Kind of a Big Deal
on the Internet

It's kind of cool how anyone can create a community online and make their own platform to amplify their voices. Fame has been democratized, and almost anyone can become famous at any time for doing anything. But this celebrity potential has also created monsters amongst us, and I'm probably in that number.

The new superstars can be bloggers, Viners, YouTubers, and other digital influencers who built their platforms purely from social media and the work they've done online. We are getting endorsement deals, movie roles, and elevation because of our online presence, but sometimes people take whatever this Internet fame thing is too seriously and lose all perspective and humility. This is why I'm judging those of us who are big deals on the Internet. Too many of us have bought into our own hype. Let's talk about the types of online celebs you can find.

The Number Dropper: This is the person who cannot go an entire conversation without talking about their social-media numbers and huge following. They will drop their whole media kit at your feet during random conversation, and you wonder if they want a cookie or a high five from you. You could be at brunch talking about how you want your eggs scrambled hard with cheese, and they'll mention how they have half a million fans on Facebook. Congratulations, but do you want the omelet or the pancakes? We need you to order already because we're starving and this is a meal, not a social-media conference. Relax, okay?

The Brand: This person takes the idea of themselves as a "brand" to heart, and I don't know if they talked to a wack social-media strategist, but they think being "on brand" means *always* doing the thing they're known for, no matter in what context or how ridiculous they come off. If they have a "thing" online, they will make sure to do it in real life, too. There's on brand, and then there's being a walking cartoon. Are you wearing the same thing all day every day because it's what you're known for online? Are you Bart Simpson? Doug Funny? I just described myself, I know. I do love me some blazers and red pumps. But some folks are so bad about this that you think they're under contract to wear that yellow flower in their hair every day, or white pants all year long. Do they get fined for being seen in something different? Why are they so dedicated to their look? Do they think people won't know who they are without it? Why are you wearing your famous fur beanie *to a beach*? You look sweaty as hell. Take that off!

The Quasi-famous: There comes a time when you earn your "I'm a digital influencer" badge by someone recognizing you on the street. They might come up to you excitedly and ask to take a selfie with you. Hopefully, you at least ask what their name is. The first time it happens, you walk away either freaked out or really excited because someone you've never met in real life was super-happy to see you. Well, some of our eCelebs will take this first time to heart.

They got recognized for their video or blog once, and now they're all "I live in fear of being recognized everywhere." Girl, bye. ONE person seeing you does not make you Princess Diana. This person is really insufferable if you go somewhere with them, because they're looking around for people who might recognize them, so they make that lingering eye contact that creeps folks out. One day, you're standing on the street with them when someone interrupts your convo. Quasi-famous jumps to conclusions and goes, "Yes, we can totally take a selfie," and the person is all, "Oh, I was just wondering if you knew where Main Street is." At that moment, if you listen real close, you can hear a small ripping noise, because their ego just got torn in two.

What is also hilarious is when they assume that because their video/blog/Snap got some high number of views means *everyone* they come across has seen it. There is nothing funnier than when someone tells someone else, "You've probably seen my video," and the other person responds with a blank stare and says, "No, I haven't. Can you tell me about it? How do I find it?" I relish those times, and I'm sitting there looking back and forth like I'm at a petty tennis match. They say things like, "You've probably read my post on . . ." Actually, I have not. Don't assume anything. Even if I have, I might still tell you I haven't just because I want to humble you.

The Powerful Threatener: Online influence does not always translate to people giving a damb in real life. But the Powerful Threatener doesn't understand this. They go to dinner, board a plane, or drop off their clothes at the dry cleaner expecting perfect service. When they don't receive it, they will pull out their "I'm famous on the Internet" chip quickly, saying things like, "I am so going to put you on blast on Twitter and Facebook and my blog." It's too bad no one curr. Sit down. It's especially funny when the person they're threatening has no Internet knowledge. "You're going to bust me on Facetweet?" They could not give any less of a damb.

Join the mere mortals down here, and talk to a manager if the service sucks. Stop threatening people with your abstract fame.

The Mismatched: They are known for being direct, brash, and loud online. They tell it like it is, and they do it when they want. Then you meet them in a social setting and they're wallflowers who look uncomfortable being where they are. Also, they spend the entire time on their phone, and then you log on to Twitter and see that they're posting up a storm like they're the middle of the party. Is the persona not real? Are you tired that day? The flip side is the person who is real thoughtful and quiet online, but an asshole in real life—the online feminist dude who calls women bitches casually when he's out, or the Christian values–preaching video blogger whose marriage is only monogamous when his wife is looking.

The Revolutionary: This eCeleb is notorious for their social justice–driven platform. They are brilliant as hell, their work is dope, and they take themselves very seriously. As they should, of course. Except you cannot have a conversation at brunch with them without the words "respectability," "rendered invisible," and "paradigm" being used. Their burdens got burdens, and you wonder if they'll need a back brace, since they seem to shoulder every single problem in the world all by themselves. I know you were on *The Melissa Harris-Perry Show* twice, but can I just eat my breakfast trio in peace? Also, can you take your Gloria Steinem book off the table? We need that space for more orange juice, which you are more pressed than. The funny thing is that you knew them back when they would call people all types of names but "child of God." Now, you cannot tell them anything, because they ended up on one too many lists of "45 About That Life Activists You Should Know." Their best work is preaching to the choir using insider language all day on Twitter.

The Pioneer: This person believes that all great ideas on the Internet originated in their mind. They've threatened to quit social media because they think everyone is biting their brilliance, and they put a ᵀᴹ next to everything they tweet, even though it's a regular-ass phrase that people have been using for years. The thing about the Pioneer is that you can't tell them shit. You cannot tell them that their wit is just them regurgitating other people's words that they forgot they heard before. They spend most of their time pursuing people who have "stolen" from them, yet they have no real leg to stand on. You wonder whether if they spent more of their time actually doing work they wouldn't think someone else using a phrase from 1972 was worth losing hours of their day to. Also, they are prone to quote themselves from time to time, or create memes of their own "deep words."

* * *

I've actually described myself in a couple of these profiles. Now I'm ashamed and judging myself for being an asshole. It is all fickle, and those follower numbers do not feed most people, do not guarantee sustained notoriety, and surely do not mean everyone is cheering for you. Internet fame is flimsy, because it can be erased with the press of a button in some tech guy's office. Those of us who think we've earned our own fame have to realize that we've more than likely done it in a walled garden that is out of our control. People have had their Facebook pages with 500,000 fans deleted for violating some terms they cannot comprehend. People have been suspended from Twitter accounts with 200,000 followers. We need to keep in mind how ephemeral all of this is.

We should check ourselves a bit and understand that being a big deal on the Internet is not necessarily permanent, and being a "new age" celebrity can be fleeting. You are only as good as your last piece of work.

On Sex Tapes

 We are human beings, and we are supposed to have sex because it keeps us going, literally. We are programmed for sex, and God made it feel good so we'd want to do it. Praise Him everlasting. But we are terrible about talking about sex, we are shy about admitting we watch other people have sex, and we live in ways contradictory to our natural inclinations. We're hypersexual prudes, which makes no sense. When we see others having sex on tape, we automatically label them as deviant. But we watch those same tapes over and over again, not admitting that we're actually studying and learning from them. So when nude pictures leak, and sex tapes drop, and porn flourishes, we frown, as if they do not exist because we like to consume them.

The existence of homemade sex tapes is neither new nor extraordinary. Maybe folks just want to see what their own "OMG, I'm coming" face looks like. I don't even like hearing my own voice on the radio, but no judgment, okay? Do what you gotta do. Most people keep these tapes for their personal collection, to be studied and reminisced about and to get your cookies off on a night when you're bored at home. Some people will make the decision to release these tapes for public consumption to make money and to try to get famous from it. I think that's fine, as long as they know what will come of that and they are realistic about their end game.

In the past, sex tapes were often leaked by vengeful, butthurt-ass exes who wanted to publicly humiliate their partners. Those people deserve a special ride on the express train to hell for willingly violating the agreement of partnership and broadcasting such intimate moments for vengeance. I need Satan to add extra gasoline to their fireplaces every night when they get to their apartments in Hades. I am not judging the folks who had to suffer through that. I am side-eyeing the people who have started using sex tapes as part of their blueprint to becoming notorious.

When does it make sense to release a sex tape on your way to fame? If you want to be famous for doing porn. Or if you want to be a worldwide teacher of sex workshops. As long as your goal is to be known for sex, then yes, drop a tape on the people and flourish. But many of those who have willingly let their sex game become public property are not trying to become the next non-political Deep Throat or Supahead. They just want their names to be known by any means necessary, and I'm judging anyone who uses that strategy for lacking self-awareness and a realistic outlook on our society.

The game was changed when Kim Kardashian's sex tape dropped and overnight, she went from being Paris Hilton's closet cleaner to a known quantity. Kim is the godmother of Sex Tape Success, but those who want to follow her map aren't taking into account that she is an exception, far from the rule. She broke the mold, and no one has been able to replicate her feat. Many have come before and after her, but few have sustained their relevance as she has. Her current position and relevance in our popular culture has given false hope to folks, and I want us to close that Pandora's box. Leave hope right in there, because this ain't the way.

Less than a decade ago, Kim was a sidekick to someone else who had no real talent but was famous anyway (Paris Hilton). Now, she's one of the most famous people on earth (with the most followers on Instagram to prove it), and she's married to one of the biggest rock stars on the planet (Kanye West). Her come up is so real that it gives me vertigo. It is impressive how much the woman has kept her name in these streets, having done nothing extraordinary professionally or artistically.

She started by selling sex, and she continues that in a way by letting her body do the talking for her. She is still selling sex, but she is no longer doing it quite so literally. She just posts pics of her ample backside on her social media to remind us. For your sex tape to lead to success, you have to use your ass as your brand perpetually. Can people attempt to change the conversation about themselves? Sure, they can. But Kim rolled with the tide and rode the sex wave all the way to the bank.

You will need to place pictures of yourself wearing onesies and nothing else on Instagram, with your ass to the camera. You will need to attempt to break the Internet by being on the cover of a magazine slathered in oil with your ass crack as the focus of the shot. You have to be self-aware and know that you are offering nothing else of value besides a beat face and a bangin' ass, and you have to serve that on a platter constantly. And because you've based all your public worth on your looks, you'll be pressured into keeping it perfect, so you'll need to chop and screw it with plastic surgery to make sure no parts are ever out of place. If they are, you might be cast out of the circle of fame quick, fast, and in a hurry.

Kim has done it by playing right into these facts, not attempting to offer much else of value besides that beat face and bangin' ass. Of course, you keep using your body as your *only* tool of value and people might continue to see you as a simpleton who's dragging two watermelons behind you, with an echoing space between your ears. In all things, be clear what your messaging is. Any woman who wants to try to be like Kim can choose to do so. Choose your choice, and all that jazz. However, our society has not gotten its shit together enough to allow such a choice to lead to prosperity most of the time.

Building your career on a sex tape is fine if you understand that it will define you. People love to categorize things. It is natural, and once you've done a sex tape, folks' brains place you in the porn-star category with quickness. Thereafter, people seeing you as anything but that sexual object will not compute. It's unfair, unjust, and seemingly unchanging, unfortunately. So no, you can't drop a sex tape today and expect that it means you'll get new clients all of a sudden for your finance-consulting company. That is not how that will work. Getting famous from a sex tape means you will live in that shadow for a long time. You might cure cancer, but the asterisk next to your name will mention the sex tape you did in 1952.

Almost a decade later, Kim can break the mold because she has an entire machine behind her committed to ensuring that she remains in the limelight. Her mother, who is the chief strategist of turning shady shit into shining glory, has created and executed the plan smoothly, because many years after that tape, Kim is still commanding our attention. She is being forced down our throats at every turn, and her every blink is news. She is making millions on video games, she's been on the cover of *Vogue*, and she steps on red carpets and shuts them down.

Paris Hilton's sex tape was leaked and it damaged her name and her brand. It ostracized her from her very famous family name, and it ruined her journey to the top. Her former assistant is making millions on a video game and ending up on the cover of major magazines, while Paris is appearing on red carpets and being elbowed out the way for Miley Cyrus. I think it comes down to Kim's commitment to stay in the limelight, a mom who isn't afraid to pimp her assets out, and an entire family that is equally as pressed for notoriety. She went from a sex tape to a reality TV show that was spurred on by her love of getting married and her aversion to having moments of privacy. That show then spawned a variety of other business enterprises for her. Seriously impressive.

If you want to be famous, there are other shortcuts to take. If you want to sell sex, find a skill to go along with that, so at least you sell sex AND something else, like music. Or art. I don't know. And if you release a sex tape, please have some tricks up your sleeve. At least do something interesting, so we can try to learn something as we watch your pre-orgasm face. I've sat through some boring videos where not only was I mad that I let my computer almost get a virus but I would have gotten more excited from watching people mark down prices on amazing shoes. Are you really gonna do missionary the entire time? I need someone to contort themselves so bad they almost get a charley horse halfway through so I know it's real.

People used to aspire to be famous *for* something. Now they just want to be famous, without it mattering how they get that fame, but all notoriety is not created equal. It is not enough to want your name in the lights if the bulb is covered by the dust of the desperation that got you there.

The Unreal World

I relish trashy TV. Lord knows I do. I salivate when I find out a new season of my favorite reality television show is about to air, because the petty in me appreciates the guaranteed drama I am going to be consuming. All that performance, in one-hour spurts, and it's coming from regular people and celebrities alike. Yes, count me in for a watch! But it's a guilty pleasure because as I watch it, I am acutely aware that our culture does not benefit from glorifying these bad decisions by broadcasting them everywhere. Some people loiter and eat kale to contribute to the detriment of society. I watch bad TV. I consider us even.

Back in ancient times (aka 1992), a show premiered on MTV called *The Real World*. Seven strangers in their twenties, of different backgrounds, sexual orientations, and classes, were thrown together in a house for six months, with cameras on them 24/7. Their every movement was captured and edited into twenty-two episodes that attempted to show their experience as completely as possible. Six entire months were edited down to twenty-two hours, but what ended up airing was compelling storytelling.

Their joys, conflicts, and frustrations were laid out, and we saw people form real relationships with each other. The show's tagline was "When people stop being polite and start getting real." *The Real World* was groundbreaking TV. In the second season, Tami decided to have an abortion and became the first woman to openly discuss that decision in primetime. Pedro, from season three, was the first gay man on TV to talk about being HIV-positive. Ruthie, from season eight, had an intervention and was sent to rehab for her alcohol problem after driving drunk. The show tackled real issues, and in the drama that played out, people at home saw themselves and their struggles.

We did not have a category for it then, but *The Real World* was quite possibly the grandfather of reality TV. From where it started to where it currently is, the genre has devolved. It is now a stop on every fame whore's express train to rock bottom, and I am judging us for allowing it to be a complete spectacle. There is nothing left of "reality" in reality TV, and yet it's taken over our idea of what entertainment is.

I don't know if any show since the early seasons of *The Real World* has been able to capture the authenticity of people coexisting without preset agendas. What made that show special was that because there had been none like it before, people did not have expectations of how to behave, what would get more them airtime, and what would happen. There were no templates, so people were mostly themselves, albeit the camera-edited versions. Some of the cast members on *The Real World* were able to parlay their time on the show into disc jockey jobs and other on-air personality work. Then it became clear that this reality TV thing could actually be a catalyst for some type of fame, no matter how fleeting. Shows like *Survivor* got bigger, and even the people who got voted off never went fully offscreen. There was always a reunion show or something else for them to come back to. When folks figured out that they could actually use appearances on these shows to get their names out there, reality TV started going to shit.

Networks realized how few resources they needed to put into these programs, and how big the return on their small investment could be. You didn't need writers, multiple sets, and all the expenses you had for a scripted show, but you could get the same ratings? Bingo. Then they started upping the ante on the shenanigans, because people love trash, and the more drama there is, the more eyes they'd get. All of this basically led reality TV to the dumpster level of quality it now inhabits.

Reality TV is now about getting people to behave badly under manufactured circumstances with instigated drama. The level of sensationalism is constantly being increased. I remember when people would be kicked off shows for making violent physical contact with anyone, castmates or otherwise. Many people remember the Slap Heard Around the World on season six of *The Real World*, when Stephen reached into the car to slap Irene as she was leaving. I can recall the sound his palm made connecting with her face, and I was like, GAHTDAMB. My feelings were hurt for homegirl, because it was such a sucka-ass thing for him to do. That was scandalous back then, and he rightly got kicked off the show for it.

If that were to happen now, not only would Stephen get more airtime, but he'd get a whole segment in the reunion show where he'd talk about how he'd do it again in a heartbeat. Irene might come running onstage, get her retaliatory hit in before producers pulled her off him. They'd let her go, as if she'd really calmed down, and then act surprised when she lunged at him again.

People have never been saints on these shows, but at least before, their conflicts were relatively organic. Now, people behave badly on reality TV because they are being told to, pushed to, or tacitly encouraged to. Adults are being told to act a complete fool on camera so they can get a dramatic clip for the trailer. Yes, the anger these folks feel toward each other is real, but the way the beef happens is usually the work of crafty producers and writers. Yes, these shows have writers now.

I was having a conversation with a producer who used to work for a major reality show and had quit his job. I asked why. He said, "One day, after sitting through a two-hour production meeting where we strategized on how to make one of the women hate the other so they could get into a fight on camera, I came home and asked myself what I was doing for a living."

Let that sink in. There was a strategy meeting to create situations that would make two people actively despise each other. Holy shit, we're the pits. How did we get here? Nobody's supposed to be here. I asked him if the people are ever privy to the puppet-mastering, and he says absolutely. They fall into the trap anyway, because they know that if they do not do it, another castmate will, and that castmate will get more airtime.

So you would willingly get into a fight with someone else because you don't want the shine off you? I do not subscribe to the "all publicity is good publicity" theory, because people are ruining their lives and chances at future careers, livelihoods, and relationships that do not require them to be human volcanoes that could blow at any moment. Most adults do not flip over tables at a restaurant when they are angry at their dining companions. Most stable, well-functioning people do not slam bottles on other people's heads because they didn't like the words they used. (Yes, this really happened on TV.) These shenanigans are phony, and people are being caught up in the web of lies, all because they think it will make them famous.

Then again, we gotta realize that twenty-six women, over two seasons, went on a show to compete for the love of Flavor Flav, a man who reminds me of a termite, was already partnered up in real life, and had a gajillion kids by many different women. People willingly went and competed for his approval on national television. I want to say they looked past all that to see the heart of him, but the benefit skipped out and doubt took over. The women who chose to be on that show did so because they thought it would get them some ounce of acclaim, when it mostly got them ridicule and embarrassment. I do think one of them got a janky lip balm endorsement deal out of it. And possibly a new wig.

Despite how terrible it was, I watched that show faithfully, along with many others that were shameless in their foolery enthusiasm. These shows feed my love of all things dramatic at someone else's expense, because there is a 98.2 percent chance of ample cussing, fights, and tears. Those of us who watch do it partly because we love feeling superior to other people. We might not want to admit it, but we love seeing that others are living worse than we are. We love trash and we revel in this virtual wasteland on our TVs.

On *Here Comes Honey Boo Boo*, we got to see the daily lives of a poor country family and their husky daughter with pageant dreams. When the matriarch lets the kids eat Cheetos for breakfast and ours just had cereal (full of marshmallows and sugar), we feel good about our decisions. We've fed our kids different poison in a somewhat more acceptable package, but they got paid $1,500 per episode for their fails.

One of the problems with our unending appetite for these shows is they constantly have to raise the bar for foolishness. There is a show for everything now, and the level of scrutiny that some people let the general public have over their personal lives is mind-boggling. Entire marriages become show fodder. Counseling and therapy sessions for serious issues are taped and disseminated for our entertainment. Celebrities are using reality TV to add to their publicity portfolios, which can backfire spectacularly. We've seen time and time again how famous people's shows have turned their reputations upside down. When you find out your favorite singer or actress is living a life in shambles, even worse than you are, they fall off their pedestal. Even our political process feels like a reality TV show; debates are playing out like reunion specials, and the person whose zinger against their opponent lands the best usually wins. We got dudes in raggedy squirrel hairhats running for president of the United States while acting like characters on the worst competition show you've ever seen.

We exploit children, lovers, heartache, family members, poverty—anything and everything. We even exploit death. Three months after a major icon died, her family had a reality TV show airing where we got to see them grapple with the loss of the larger-than-life lady. This makes me assume that TWO months after she passed, they were already signing up for the show. Sixty days. Eight weeks. That feels like nothing. That's no time to really deal with the sudden death of a loved one. In fact, I had barely gotten over it at that point, and I didn't even know her personally! It was too soon, especially when cameras followed them as they went to visit her grave for the first time. It felt crass. It was one train wreck that I felt uneasy about watching, because it was the epitomization of what is wrong with this reality-TV culture we now live in. We were supposed to be entertained, but it felt so dirty that we had turned what should have been this incredibly personal process into an aquarium exhibit, with humans in the tank. I was embarrassed both for her family and for those of us who tuned in.

We are scraping the bottom of the decency barrel when a woman can be watching her favorite medical reality show and see her husband die right on her screen. Yes, this happened. A woman in New York lost her husband after he was struck by a truck. While tuning in to the medical reality show *NY Med* one day, a story line that felt vaguely familiar played out in front of her eyes. Except this was not some fiction. She watched as doctors tried to save her husband, heard his cries of pain and how he called out for her. She watched as the doctors said he was coding and as they pronounced him dead. She hadn't known that his death had been filmed, and certainly not for a reality TV show. COMME DES FACKONS![19] Did the dying man sign a waiver between being wheeled into the

---

[19]*comme des fackons*: Because "come the fuck on" doesn't have the same ring to it.

ER and losing his life? How is that okay? How are we so parched for drama that we've reached the point where watching people die is actually considered entertainment? And let's not fool ourselves. This is purely for entertainment. It is not to enlighten or educate. It is to pull us in, captivate us, and leave us wanting more.

Reality TV shows also reinforce dangerous stereotypes and tropes. These shows turn people into caricatures of the sassy Black woman, the dirty hillbilly, the voguing gay best friend. They are all there, filling their roles and adding to all our issues. What do they have in common? They want to be known. They don't consider the downside. Once they've been branded as the character they were cast for and edited into, that shadow follows them.

People have to realize that the Bethenny Frankel and Nene Leakes model of success is like hitting the lotto. It is rare! Reality TV does not catapult most people to lasting financial success— unless you're Kim Kardashian, whose mom needs to teach a graduate-level course on turning PR crises into prosperity. Most people do not go from fighting on a show to singing on Broadway. Most people do not get to turn their presence on *For the Love of Fuckshit* or *Real Housewives of No Behaviorland* into multimillion-dollar retail empires. For every Omarosa, there are a thousand Tecks. Who? Exactly.

People think they can act a fool, maybe turn it into a spin-off show, and pray that their dreams of stardom come true. The desperation that comes with wanting fame by any means necessary is alarming, because those types of folks will sell their own mamas for that "fame."

I still watch reality TV shows, but not as much as I used to. Even my quota for ratchetness felt overfilled. I actually got to a point where the formula got boring, and I knew I wasn't missing anything. I could put the TV on mute and get the same information. I just needed to look up every fifteen minutes to catch some conflict.

Reality TV has taken our penchant for voyeurism and given us options for our preferred type of foolishness to tap into. Our appetite for this kind of entertainment is as telling about us as anything else. If we were to create a time capsule of this era for future generations to discover, we'd certainly need to include footage of people breaking bottles over each other's heads over dinner. In medieval times, people would go watch people fight and make spectacles of themselves. Reality programming has become our jousting field. The knights on horses are women in too-tight dresses wearing nighttime makeup at high noon. The winner is whoever can drag the other farthest by her weave before security catches her. Everything is a circus, everyone is the bearded lady, and everyone—audience included—plays a role in this clown show.

Epilogue: Do Something That Matters

When I was about three or four, I had this baby doll that was my absolute favorite thing in the world. She was brown, had short hair, and looked so real it was almost freaky. I was totally her fake mom, and I'd cuddle her and have her sleep next to me and everything. One day, a woman who went to high school with my mom came to visit. She brought her daughter, who was also my age, and we got along fine, until she wanted to play with my baby doll and I was all, "Hands off!" Because sharing this thing I loved was not an option. She ran to her mother crying, and I was looking like, "What's that got to do with me?" Before they left, my mom told me to hand my doll over to homegirl, and I looked at her like she had just told me candy was a figment of my imagination. Mom took my doll from me and handed it to the girl, and I hit the first wall-slide I can remember. I wept. The girl's mother tried to hand the doll back to little distraught me, but my mom told her no, it was

HER gift. THE HELL IT IS. I DIDN'T SIGN OFF ON THIS. I didn't scrawl on anybody's release form.

After they left, my mom came over to the sobbing me and said, "I know you really liked that doll, but that little girl does not have as much as you have. You should give if you have more than you need. Also, you have other toys to play with." PSHT. WHATEVER, LADY! YOU JUST STOLE MY JOY.

I mean, she didn't have to illustrate the power of giving by handing over my favorite toy *in the world*, but I get it. I remember that after I wept bitterly for a couple of minutes, I was okay. (Relatively. The fact that I still remember the story means I continue to harbor some butthurtness about it.) I grew up to be a well-rounded (ha!) adult who is pretty functional. But who knows what having that doll did for that little girl? Who knows what impact it had?

Her selflessness is one of the things I admire the most about my mother. It is why I'm here. Well, she GAVE me life (the ultimate gift—thanks, Mom!), but most importantly, she's given me a sense of obligation to serve. She didn't tell me I need to give away all my favorite things, but the lesson was that I need to serve even when it's inconvenient, especially when relinquishing what I have in surplus is a mild annoyance at worst.

I fear that too many of us think of giving back as an option instead of an obligation, and I judge some of us for not being brave enough to commit to being truly beneficent.

I have never had to worry about where my next meal is coming from, or if I'm going to have a roof over my head tonight, or if the clothes on my back will suffice to keep me warm. And for that, I am richer than 75 percent of the people in the world. This is why I feel like we're failing at existence. The fact that my having the most basic things I need makes me an exception, rather than the rule, is how I know we are not doing enough for mankind. There are still children who are starving, or homeless. And kale is an accepted vegetable that people pay to eat. We've gone wrong somewhere, folks.

It can be overwhelming when we think of all that is wrong around us, and these thoughts can cripple us into just trying to make sure we're okay ourselves, day by day. Finding our own happiness and contentment can be revolutionary all by itself. This I know. I encourage everyone to find their own footing.

Nevertheless, I am a big believer in the notion that we've each got to look outside ourselves and figure out what we're going to do to make this world a little bit less terrible. Even though I check Craigslist several times a week to see if Mars has gotten its shit together and is looking for new roommates, we're currently all stuck here on Earth together. (I figure if Bitcoin exists, then surely we must be close to creating a colony on the red planet.) So while we're here on the planet with water and perfect conditions that allow us to exist, what are we doing to contribute to it? What are we doing to ensure that the third rock from the sun isn't a hellhole where everything sucks? Are we just using up oxygen and giving nothing back besides our trash?

Some of us are in better positions to be able to give our time, money, voices, and power to making the world a better place (for you and me and the entire human race). There are far too many people whose very survival is an act of revolution as they remain here against all odds. The very fact that they're standing and walking and talking and being is worthy of awe. On the other hand, there are also plenty of us who are in positions to give something, say something, or do something that can make one small ripple of good change.

Sometimes, we feel the pressure and self-imposed expectation that when we do something, it needs to be big and perfect. That can render us useless and ensure that we do nothing because we're so afraid of not doing enough. That's tapping out before we begin. Damb that. I am here to tell us all to drop that. Small acts can go far, so you thinking you cannot do enough is not okay. You can, and I am asking you to at least try.

You do not have to be Captain Planet or Batman. No one is

expecting you to save Gotham from the Joker. But you also cannot just be the person being saved constantly and not saving those behind you.

Doing nothing of service is like someone throwing you a rope to pull you out the water, and then when you get safely in the boat you pull the rope up behind you instead of helping others who are still doggy-paddling for their lives. To me, that is what we're doing when we are in positions of power or have platforms and do nothing of note with them. Odds are the reason we even have the opportunity to be on those pedestals is because of the work of someone who came before us. Choosing not to maximize our positive impact is careless.

I'm not asking you to donate millions (unless you got it), or protest for forty days (unless that's the life you're about), or write a book about making the world a better place (unless you really want to). I am asking each of us to examine our lives, see where we've lucked out, and try to make someone else's path easier than ours.

There are certain things that have placed some of us in positions of authority, power, wealth, and extra well-being. We've come upon, earned, or been born into trust funds, or the talent that makes people on the street know who we are, or asses that won't quit (hey, J.Lo!), or we're in the default majority group and have a leg up in this world. Either way, there are enough of us who are privileged in one way or another. What are we doing with the elevation we've been given?

Good question you didn't ask. I wholeheartedly believe that adage of "to whom much is given, much is required." In whatever way you can, do something to lift someone else up. One of the easiest ways to do that? Be an ally, by living in ways that respect others who are marginalized.

You're white? Get some Black friends. Know what racism is and how you are a part of it. Don't use the N-word (even if it's in your favorite song). Denounce the system, and acknowledge your privilege. Don't rock blackface.

You're a man? Treat women like they're equal beings. Don't rape them. Don't hit them. Don't harass them. When they're being disrespected and you see it, speak up. When your buddies are making "bitch" jokes, don't laugh. You should even tell them that shit isn't funny.

You're straight? Love people, no matter who they choose to love. Don't treat your gay friends as accessories. Don't use or stay silent when someone else uses derogatory language. Don't try to pray someone's gay away.

You're able? Invite your friends with disabilities to places where they will not struggle to enter or exist. Teach your children that different isn't synonymous with subpar. Raise kids who have seen you lead by example. Let them know that to be a good person means embracing all people, even those whose normal may be different from others'.

If you start there, you're doing something decent. At the minimum, you won't be contributing too much to the many shitty systems of oppression in this world. That's huge.

But those of us who can do more than just merely NOT being extra shitty should do more by consciously giving back. Again, it is not about donating money to a disaster-relief fund if you don't have it. Sometimes, it can be as simple as speaking up about the crappy state of affairs around us.

For me, it is really important for people to have a platform that they use for more than fluff. What is the point of having access to millions of people when all you're doing is talking about yourself? It is selfish, it is narrow, and it is a disservice to the power you have. Wield it for more than promoting your work. I want to dropkick some people off their pedestals, because they're standing up there and doing nothing to pull people up with them.

You might not be an expert on a topic, but your willful silence on an issue that affects the very people who are responsible for putting money in your pocket is complicity. The community that is responsible for your elevation should not be getting murdered, injured, or oppressed without you at least bearing witness that this oppression exists. Your silence is complicity, and your lack of giving a damb is pure bullshit. Sure, you're not obligated to. Sure, the only thing you *need* to do is stay Black (or white, or whatever) and follow the drinking gourd to the Lord one day. Oh, and you have to pay taxes. But besides that, you're not *required* to do a freaking thing.

However, the lack of requirement does not mean you shouldn't feel like it is your duty to use your voice or your platform or your power for something greater than or beyond yourself. Obligation and ethics are often mutually exclusive, but that doesn't mean they should not work in tandem from time to time.

Many of us have a clear purpose: to entertain the masses. This is what we get paid for, and it is what we delight in. But as we make people laugh, we can still make them think critically. The most prolific, revolutionary comedians are the ones who dare to use their humor to satirize the world around them in order to highlight where we need to do better. They might poke fun, but underlying the humor is important commentary about our world.

It's not easy. Most things worth doing aren't. The times when it is most uncomfortable for us to speak up are usually when our voices are most needed and when what we need to say is most important. Why? Because it's hard to stand and speak truth to power when it comes to anything that is not trivial. When our voices shake, that's when the words need to be heard the most. We are all different, with various backgrounds and opinions that span the colors of the rainbow. We will not always agree. What we feel we need to say will not always be palatable. The systems in place depend on us playing by the rules, so rocking the boat is not fun. However, if you're in one boat, and you see another capsizing but you do nothing to help when you are able, how do you sleep at night? Maybe it's not up to you to save those people, but at least blow a whistle to give them a fighting chance. Also, the ocean scares me, and I'm totally wearing a life vest right now just in case. Technically, I can swim, but knowing water is deeper than I am tall makes me freeze up. Just thought you should know.

Privilege comes in many forms, and being popular is one of them. Having a platform and a listening audience and immediate access to a big group of people is certainly something that most people do not have. Those of us with these platforms, whether we are writers or entertainers, are in positions of power. How we choose to use our social endowment is up to every individual, of course. However, I bristle at those who are so concerned with their "brand" that they will only ever talk about that narrow thing they're known for. People are afraid of ruffling feathers, but sometimes the fear isn't worth the shutting up. Also, people don't give their fans enough credit. An audience needs to see those they support as whole people, not a bunch of one-topic-spewing robots. When shit hits the fan, and people in positions of authority and positions with access don't speak out, everybody loses. How can you passively sit on your high horse when the barn is crumbling around you?

Many of my fellow bloggers, writers, and content creators have niches. We have been told over and over again that we prosper and flourish when we pick a lane and stick to it. We have been told that our audience likes to know what box we're in, and when we veer away from that box, we are giving people the unexpected and they won't appreciate it. Well, I disagree that bloggers should not sometimes switch lanes, even if just for a moment. I cannot ignore what's happening around me because I'm afraid to alienate readers. If the audience I've built leaves because I talk about what is important to me, I got the wrong people. There's always a threat of backlash or loss of money from speaking up. I get it. I'm a professional troublemaker and loudmouth. I have pissed people off many times. I've probably pissed people off with this very book, but it's worth it to me to take personal risks for public gain.

Speaking up for what you believe in does not look the same for everyone. Being a concerned human is not some uniform behavior that we must all practice. For me, it is the simple acknowledgement of injustice. It is the act of stating that you see it and you do not condone it. It is the refusal to ignore the world's shenanigans in an effort to be neutral. Neutrality is for suckas, and it does nothing but indicate that you are all right with bad things happening. It is like watching someone get robbed and not even calling 911. You just sit there and watch as if real people aren't being harmed.

When you speak out, someone else might be encouraged to do the same. Do not be silent. You do not have to be a crusader, but someone else's battle could easily become your own. A fire burning down your neighbor's house could easily spread to yours. Acting like it's not your fight doesn't make it so.

There are those of us who run our own businesses, or who write on our own websites, or aren't living paycheck to paycheck. Those of us who are not in acute danger of losing our livelihoods can take more risks. We can make more mistakes. We can stand even when sitting is safer. I ask that we be the first ones to do so, in place of those who cannot.

I am not asking everyone to be activists. I am not asking everyone to march on the front lines. I am not asking every writer, public figure, or celebrity to lead social movements. I am not asking them to make speeches on how they have a dream. I am, however, challenging people to not stay silent as the world crumbles. You do not have to yell. Even a whisper of truth matters in an echo chamber of lies.

Cicely Tyson, the Matron Saint of Everything Amazing, once said, "In my early years, there were a number of experiences that made me decide I could not afford the luxury of just being an actress. There were a number of issues I wanted to address. And I wanted to use my career as a platform." That quote makes me fist pump, and it makes me look around and wonder why that type of courage cannot be more common. Are we living the lowered-expectations life when we expect otherwise? Probably. And the idealist in me would like to see more.

Money cannot absolve people from the moral obligation of condemning atrocities, but if people do choose to be silent, I hope they are at least using their good fortune to speak for them. Speaking up is not the only way to use your influence. Some people are privileged to be in the top 1 percent. Some are just lucky enough not to be drowning in debt or living in constant fear of financial fallout. Money is power, and it can be wielded to make change, even when the person who has it is silent. There are folks who are lacking for nothing and sitting on millions. What do you do with that after you buy all the yachts, go on all the vacations, splurge on every piece of clothing, and sock away enough to leave your children comfortable? There is only so much money you can spend in a lifetime, so what will you do with it? When your kids' kids are set financially, what else should you do besides give some of it away?

I have never seen a check with more than five zeros on it, so I cannot even fathom the amount of money some people have, and what goes into parceling it out. I know it exists, though. And I have some ideas for how to spend it: Write some checks for charity. Find worthy causes that you've researched and give them money. Find an afterschool program to support. Fund medical research to cure an illness. Listen. When you die, you cannot take it with you. You might as well find something useful to do with it here.

There are multiple ways to use your influence for something that matters. Some yell, some march, some teach, some sing, some give, some volunteer. You're famous and known and feel like you're having unfair expectations thrust upon you? Well, yeah. You're right. But again, from those to whom much is given, much is required. It's kind of the fee you have to pay for being at the top.

We are not just affected by the issues that touch us directly. The rich should be fighting for the poor. The healthy should be fighting for the sick. The privileged should be fighting for the oppressed. If the people who support you are being hurt every single day, and you turn your back because the pain has nothing to do with you, then you are taking their very presence for granted.

If you have a microphone plugged into an amplifier, it is wrong for you not to sing. If you have been placed in a sphere of influence, I believe that it is wrong for you not to use it to better the world. If you do not feel like it is your duty to leave this place better than you found it, then you're taking everything around you for granted. Don't squander your social currency. Don't squander your wealth. And if some people stop supporting your work because you dared to do something about a shitty world, good riddance to bad things and assholes!

Shirley Chisolm said, "Service to others is the rent you pay for your room here on earth." Some of us are mad delinquent on this rent. We owe back pay, but that's okay. We just need to start now. We can start doing better any time we want.

Acknowledgments

OMG, I WROTE A BOOK! Yes, I am screaming that, and now there's an Acknowledgments section so you know it's real. I wrote a freaking book, and here you are, holding it in your hands and reading my words. Thank YOU for that. Thank YOU for spending time with my work. The fact that you made it this far means we officially go together.

This is a dream come true. I hope folks don't mind that I will have "author" next to my name now, like some folks have "MD" once they become doctors. I will officially be on Team Doing the Most, and when folks try to say stuff I don't like, I'll just randomly yell "I WROTE A BOOK," even when it's not relevant.

Who do you have to blame for that? My agent, Michael Harriot of Folio Literary Agency, and my editor at Henry Holt, Allison Adler. Mike, thank you for seeing the value in my work and stepping out to represent me. I am really proud that I have now taught you what it means to be shady and how to give proper side-eye. You are welcome for the opportunity!

And Allison, thank you for trusting my vision and voice for this book. You made the process a joy, and you didn't judge me when I called you squealing when my book was officially available for preorder. I hope your ears have recovered from my gleeful hollering. You also make me realize that editors are priceless diamonds who must be cherished, because they make us writers look good. Props to the entire Henry Holt team for believing in this book.

In the times when I didn't trust my own voice, I was able to fall back on some of my mentors who I have also forced to be my friends and now they cannot get rid of me: Aliya S. King, Denene Millner, and Karen Walrond. You three pushed me forward when I wanted to stop because I didn't know if the words sucked. And many thanks to Rakia Clark for helping me make my manuscript sing when I thought it croaked!

Meanwhile, the people who will have to put up with me with my newfound importance as a Topflight Author of the World must be thanked. My family is my backbone, and I love them dearly. My mom, especially, deserves gratitude—not just because she gave me life, but because my side-eye was passed down from her. I've been on the receiving end of it all my life, and it has taught me how to also tell people to have a seat without words. I high-five heaven for my first home, Yemi. Shout-out to my sister, Kofo, my biggest cheerleader and my partner in petty. Thank you for always lifting me up. And thanks to my bro, Dele, and my sis-cuzzo, Morayo. My blood squad is amazing, man! I love y'all like Nigerians love white rice.

My chosen family is the shit, too. If you think I have no chill, you should meet my friends. Not one of them has behavior, and this is partly why I keep them around. They have allowed me to practice my shadiness over the years. But also, they celebrate with me, and our love is real. It was in Antonio's apartment that I read the e-mail saying I got my deal! Tesheena was who I called first. Toccara saw me right after I signed with my publisher. Patrice got

About the Author

LUVVIE AJAYI is an award-winning writer, pop-culture critic, and professional troublemaker who thrives at the intersection of comedy, technology, and activism. She is the person who often says what you're thinking but didn't dare to because you have a filter and a job to protect. She is also a digital strategist, noted speaker, and executive director of The Red Pump Project, a national HIV/AIDS organization.

P.S. "Ajayi" is pronounced just like it's spelled. AH-JA-YEE.